Dying to See the Light

WHY CREATION?

First Edition

Rita D Lovins

AuthorHouse™
1663 Liberty Drive
Bloomington, IN 47403
www.authorhouse.com
Phone: 1 (800) 839-8640

Published by AuthorHouse   03/06/2015

ISBN: 978-1-4969-7291-0 (sc)
ISBN: 978-1-4969-7423-5 (e)

Library of Congress Control Number: 2015903509

Print information available on the last page.

Any people depicted in stock imagery provided by Thinkstock are models, and such images are being used for illustrative purposes only. Certain stock imagery © Thinkstock.

This book is printed on acid-free paper.

KJV
Scripture quotations marked KJV are from the Holy Bible, King James Version (Authorized Version). First published in 1611. Quoted from the KJV Classic Reference Bible, Copyright © 1983 by The Zondervan Corporation.

NIV
Scripture quotations marked NIV are taken from the Holy Bible, New International Version®. NIV®. Copyright © 1973, 1978, 1984 by International Bible Society. Used by permission of Zondervan. All rights reserved. [Biblica]

CONTENTS

Foreword vii
Chapter 1   First and Second Trip
             to Heaven.................................... 1
Chapter 2   Third Trip to Heaven 22
Chapter 3   Heaven is Real......................... 28
Chapter 4   Reincarnation 37
Chapter 5   Lessons About Life.................... 53
Chapter 6   Back in My Body 60
Chapter 7   I Saw The Beauty of
             His Spirit. 70
Chapter 8   Heaven Talks Back 75
Chapter 9   Proof I Have Angels 92
Chapter 10   Forth Trip to Heaven 99
Chapter 11   Move to Mexico...................... 108
Chapter 12   Why Creation? My
             lessons begin 112
Chapter 13   I Planned My Own Life
             and Time of Death.................. 120
Chapter 14   We Are the "I AM" 133
Afterword...143

FOREWORD

Out the door I went and found myself soaring up away from the city and all I could see was a bright light of pure love and peace beckoning me. I died and had a Near Death Experience four times throughout my life. It is not easy to remember all that happened all at once over the years after crossing over. The spans between each near death experience (NDE) were filled with life. The entire story of my life is not here. The story about my near deaths is here along with the many lessons I learned while I was beyond the veil. As you read you will live through some of my experiences I enjoyed on the Heaven side of life (Beyond the Veil). If anyone had told me beforehand, I would not have believed what they were talking about. Many lessons learned were so different from what I had learned but some of the lessons were familiar.

"Heaven is real". You will learn that you are special and you are right where you are supposed to be right now. This is the perfect time for you to read this book. Included is the facts that we create our own reality and you will learn why people are born to love others of the same sex or homosexuals. When I learned why and how I came to be, I was astonished. It was so difficult to get the old teachings out of my head. The reason for the Creation of All is probably the biggest shock of everything I learned. I still spend hours contemplating what I learned. It will not sink in right away. Believe me, it takes time to come to grips to the reality of our Creation and of all that is. I learned How and Why and then what happened next.

I would like to take this time to thank all who had faith in me and helped me along this journey. My family for being so patient, for my husband George who did the laundry, dishes and generally kept the houses and apartments picked up. We did move around quite a bit. I want to especially thank everyone who helped edit this book and send me their review of this book. I would like to thank Ellen McFarland for her wonderful contribution and ideas which made this book richer.

FIRST AND SECOND TRIP TO HEAVEN

We are all butterflies. Earth is our chrysalis. We follow the fragrance from flower to flower on the Path of Eternity. Unknown

I was returning home after running away in July of 1961 at age 15. My abusive father had driven me away. My father seemed to delight in treating me like an uncontrollable wild animal that needed to be broken. I will not go into detail on this matter at this time.

I did run away to Oregon, to avoid anymore beatings. I did not want to grow up to be like my mother. She suffered from the beatings at least once a week. She was a good Catholic woman and would never think of divorce. No one in our extended family or anyone else knew what Daddy was like until after Mom's death.

I became homesick after about a year. I remembered the Christmas celebrations with my family which I missed the most during the fourteen or so months I had been away. Watching my younger siblings open their gifts on Christmas Eve was a highlight of the year. My mind dwelt in that happy time until the bus stopped in Boise, Idaho. I could not get another bus to my small home town until the next morning. I did not know Boise well so I decided to spend the night in a hotel across the street from the Greyhound station. In Oregon I had a social security card with that name so I used that to register.

The hotel was old and smelled of a musty old locker room of old dirty socks and sweaty high top gym shoes. The room had an old spring medal bed that squeaked when I sat down. A simple porcelain sink faced me from the opposite wall. The bathroom was several doors down the hall with an old fashion tub and toilet which smelled of many years of use. The bath tub had ring stains of many shades of yellow to brown, like the rings of a cut tree. The hot water was a blessing to my less than feminine smelling self. Riding a bus from the center of Oregon to Boise left me feeling grubby.

The old wood floor made eerie sounds and squeaks on my way back to the hotel room.

I simply pulled my half-slip up to cover my torso and I collapsed into bed. My dreams were strange when suddenly the door to the room flew in and I dreamed I saw a monster appeared in the doorway and pounced on me flailing his fists at my face and body. A strange strange tattoo covered his fist. Was I being wrapped in a White Light? I could not move as I faded away into oblivion with flashes of lightening seeming to fly everywhere.

I was moving through a void toward a brilliant light filled with love. I wanted to be in that light more than I had ever wanted anything before. The vibrational pull was so powerful. I joyfully allowed it to pull me. This was familiar, but from where? Did this happen to me before? It seems I was looking back.

Then I felt myself floating above watching a white 1950 Ford which began to run over a doll's head. My mother pulled the rag doll as its body spun around in her grip as she pulled the doll free of the tire just before the tire rolled completely over its head. At the moment I was soaring away through a void with people all around. They too were soaring with me. Some were faster and some slower. The brilliant light had a magnetic pull on me and I relaxed in that sweet tenderness. I had the coziest feeling I had ever experienced, even from the times my mother would hold me. The light: Oh there is the light.

I came face to face with a child who seemed to be about my age and we were playing Ring-Around-The-Rosie and she laughed with me. Then the girl said, "Do you know who I am?"

"No! But I know you from somewhere. Who are you?" I asked laughing. The joy was only as a child can experience. She took my right hand and said walk with me. I giggled with enthusiasm. I was ready to play all day.

"I am Bernie, your aunt. Come on walk with me. Hold my hand." Giggling and skipping among swirl of aromas of flowers, spices and the smell of fresh rain mixed with snowflakes. My sensory self was enjoying the most spectacular array of music, smells, feelings, and all pouring through a maze of light dancing around us. Two years ago, Blackie my little cocker *Spaniel* had eaten some poisoned meat a man had been throwing into people's yards with dogs. Blackie came up to me and ran around me barking and showing his delight of seeing me again. We played together and I picked him up and cuddled him.

"Oh, I remember now. Bernie, you died before I was born. How did you die?" I asked as we giggled and laughed together.

"I fell into the cow's water-trough and drowned. It was my time to come here."

Giggling I inquired haphazardly "Where are you? What is this place"?

She did not answer my question. We were skipping hand in hand when I felt my mother's hands on me. Then both hands were under my arm pits and she was saying, 'keep walking with me. Pick up your feet and walk'.

Blackie began to fade and I began to feel my legs walking but very unsteadily. I looked at my hand Bernie was holding and my palm was all red. Was I looking through her hand?

I felt her holding my hand all the way back to our house. The automobile accident happened just a quarter of a mile from our house. Bernie said "that doll you saw was you. You will be alright now. Good, keep walking you are doing better now" as she began to fade from my view.

I was back in my body as Mom was helping me back to our house. I wanted to go back to the light. It did not hurt there. The memory of my returning to my body stirred something within my being that brought me back. It was as if I just popped into my body through my head with a jolt.

Mom sat me in a chair as she cranked the wall-phone to call the doctor. My father came out of the bedroom asking what was going on.

I could still feel Bernie holding my hand. Then I remember sitting on my mom's lap as Daddy drove the pickup into town to the doctor's office. I was a mere six years old. "Bernie, hold my hand." Her hand was becoming lighter, fainter.

Mom bent down to my ear and asked me in a whisper, "Who are you talking to".

"Bernie, you know, your sister who died in the cow's trough" I said nonchalantly. I could feel no pain. I believed somehow Bernadette helped me be pain free.

Mom said "I never told you how Bernie died". I somehow knew her words were true. I suppose Grandma wanted to spare us grandchildren about the details of her death. Then, for a moment I had a vision of grandma crying and whaling over the death of her baby at the funeral. Grandma was so sad. I felt like holding grandma tight to sooth her grief.

I came home with a bandage around my right knee and lower leg and a cap bandage on my head. We visited grandma and grandpa later that day and I hugged grandma and told her Bernie was happy and how she played with me and held my hand. Grandma cried and I hugged her again and she just smiled and held me tight. Grandma then went to her bedroom and closed the door. Mom told me I had a piece of my scalp missing but it will grow back. When I was older I learned that a portion of the skin about 3 inches in diameter was missing and they could see my scalp.

'Where am I now? I feel sort of dizzy."

I was frolicking in the light of total love and was joined by a beautiful woman who made me think of the statue of Mary in our church. She told me it was not my time to be there and she turned me toward my limp body lying on the floor. I did not want to go so she gave me a loving, gentle push and I popped with a plunge as if into an ice cold lake through the top of my head. "Ouch" I said as I tried to focus.

I opened my eyes to a fuzzy U shaped thing nearly touching my nose. My vision began to clear and the U was hanging from a white face but there was no mouth. Where was the brilliant light I was soaring to? I was drowsy and began to realize it was not a face but was a cold white thing, but what was it? I began to move and pain racked my body. Why was I hurting so? Oh no! I was back again. No! No! No! I wanted to stay with the Light. The whole experience was so wonderful I never wanted to leave it. Why did I have to come back again?

I moved a little more and felt a groan gurgle from my throat. Puzzled I sat up and my back was against a hard medal bedstead with narrow spindles biting into my flesh. Oh! I had been under the sink. The bed had medal rods running up the foot board.

I pulled myself up and peered into the mirror above the white sink. Now I remember where I was; in the hotel room waiting for the bus. What was that in the mirror? A grotesque being with bloody matted hair and a twisted red blob. I looked down and saw my half-slip covered in blood. What happen? What was going on?

I made my way to the dim hallway through the open door. Down the hall I saw something bobbing up and down, was it a ball? No! It looked more like a head but where was the rest of the body? I began to limp toward the bobbing and a head popped up and it said, "Stop! Go back." the man behind the desk yelled. I knew I was not a pretty thing to see. Had I frightened him?

"Help me!" I finally said although my words were garbled. The pain was growing into agony.

The clerk seemed to take forever dialing the rotary phone. I bent over in pain and back tracked to my room as I felt the need to lie down before I fell down. I collapsed on the bed and drifted off into a welcome dream state.

"Miss, are you OK?" boomed the voice of a man shaking my shoulder.

Oh no! Why did he have to wake me up? The pain was beyond anything I had ever experienced, even worse than the pain from my dad when he would beat me with his belt buckle.

"Stop, it hurts!" I managed to say. There were two men dressed in white and a policeman around the bed. Soon I was on a cart being wheeled out of the room. The policeman was asking questions.

"Who did this to you young lady? How many were there?" the policeman asked several times. Did I know who they were? All I could remember was the spider web and teardrops.

"Spider web tattoo" is all I could say.

They slid me into a station wagon and the screaming of sirens hurt my ears as I moaned and cried. I could no longer hear what the men were asking. The noise seemed to stab me my head, face, nose, jaw, ribs and the rest of my body.

We finally stopped and they whisked me out of the wagon and I felt something jerk the cart. Lights were everywhere. I could no longer see the people around me, only spots from the lights. Again, the bliss of nothing enveloped me as I slipped into a stupor and beautiful lights.

I woke to a nurse in her crisp white dress and cap who was smoothing a sheet over me and pulled up a bed-rail. The pain was gone. I tried to speak but my mouth would not move. I reached up to my mouth and the nurse stopped my hand.

With a kind smile she said, "Don't touch your mouth dear. Your jaws are wired together. You have a broken lower jaw in two places. You must not disturb your jaw. You also have a broken nose with a gash that was big enough to put your finger through. Keep your hands away from the stitches."

All I knew was I was happy the pain was gone. She had mentioned something about bruised ribs but I was feeling good now.

"Here is your call light if you need anything. Don't try to get out of bed by yourself. You call me and I will help you. If you have pain I will give you another shot. Just be sure to use your call light." She left me in my wonderment of the surroundings. The walls were green just like the walls in the hospital when my little sister, Maggs had her appendix out in my home town when she was little.

I woke to a throbbing in my nose and jaw. The pulsing through my head was excruciating. I tried to sit up only to feel more pain in my ribs and abdomen.

"The call light: Where is the call light?', I thought. It was pinned to the sheet. I pushed the button as hard as I could, which created a crater in my thumb with sheer desperation. The nurse appeared in the door and came to my side

"It hurts. Please help me, it hurts," I begged.

She nodded, "I will get you a shot now!" as she pried the call button from my fist. She was gone for what seemed like an hour. I know it was only a couple of minutes. This was to be a lesson I would remember later in life.

Again, I grabbed the call light just as she came through the door with my shot. "Oh help me nurse! Please." She pulled me over and I felt the needle bite my fanny. When would the pain go away? The agony was wrenching. The next thing I remember was my nurse waking me up for a bath. She washed my face very tenderly and I realized the pain was gone. I must have fallen asleep.

A detective came to my room a couple of times gathering information about my assailant. My only description was the tattoo I saw on his hand. They said they would continue to look for who did this to me but did not hold out much luck of finding him unless he was in the system and the tattoo was registered.

I told the detective I remember what the man said to me as he was beating me: "This will teach you not to leave me standing at the Justice of the Peace. You will never have a chance to do it again." From that the detective said he believed my assailant left me for dead. "So! It was just one big man!" With that he smiled at me and turned and left my room.

I guess the man did kill me as I was in heaven rollicking with Bernie again for a short time. I wished I was back there again.

I was soon graduated to a pain pill and a large antibiotic which I had to slide to the back of my teeth and into my mouth so I could swallow water to take the pills. I still remember the pain of this process. The pain was less frequent and I was discharged from the hospital on the third day. I had to spend all my money on a bottle of pain pills and antibiotics. What was I going to do?

Then I remembered I had met Pat in Oregon during Christmas, who worked in this town. I walked to her office. I needed to find someone who could help me call my mom. I needed money to finish my trip home.

Pat, a beautiful blond woman was helpful beyond what anyone would be expected to do. She let me use her office phone to call my mother. Mom was ecstatic to hear from me. My intention had been to return home and surprise her, but now I needed her help to get home. That afternoon mom wired the money to me. It was elk hunting season and I knew Dad would be gone hunting. I wanted to return while he was away. Pat took me home with her and I slept on her couch.

The next morning Pat drove me to the bus station. During the ride down home, I saw the mountains that looked like they had been sliced off leaving flat tops which I later learned were called mesas. The Snake River wound back and forth out my window. Fond memories of my childhood flooded back. We stopped in Twin Falls and the memory of when I was two years old took me back to the day mom took me to Twin Falls to the Polio Clinic. I believe we made the trip every week, until I was walking on my own again.

One particular day we all were out on the big lawn as big as a park. I was sitting on a blanket; others were on carts, wheelchairs and standing around with crutches and braces. From the street came a cowboy on a white horse. I recognized Hopalong Cassidy and his horse Topper.

I had seen them at the movies and here they were right now. We were excited children. Hoppy talked and road. Topper skipped the big rope loop. When the show was over, Hoppy invited us to come and shake his hand and pet Topper. I wanted to pet Topper but I could not walk. Suddenly someone from behind, picked me up and put me on his lap. He was around ten years old and he wheeled me right up to the chest of Topper. I reached up and pet him. He had the softest hair I had ever felt and I remember that feeling to this day. We had horses at home but their hair was not soft like Topper's. He was a special horse.

My thoughts came back to the present as the bus entered to my home town.

Mom was waiting for me at the bus station. She hugged me so hard my jaw hurt and I had tears in my eyes. She mistook them for tears of joy and I let her because it was partly true. Mom then took me on a long trip to visit Sister Loraine, where Sister hugged me so tight the pain was almost unbearable. Sister was a dear friend of our family. The nuns came from the St. Gertrude's Academy a Benedictine Convent and school in the middle of Idaho each summer for 'Sister-School'. This was similar to vacation Bible School held in other churches. Looking back now I realized mom sent me to Catholic Boarding schools to get me away from my father. I ran away from home after the tenth grade at the St. Gertrude's. Having that time to learn to be on my own probably gave me the courage to leave home just two months after that semester ended.

Soon we were off to see relatives and friends who also hugged me until I had to take a pain pill. Mom finally realized I needed to be handled more gently to prevent the dislodging of my broken jaw. By night fall, when we arrived home I was exhausted and just wanted to sleep. Mom had cooked a stew and put some in the blender. Her home cooking was wonderful. I was happy to be home with my Mom. She made fresh juice from the vegetables in the garden. I learned then how wonderful juicing was. My brothers and sisters were home and all greeted me with vigor, except for my brother who was 2 years younger than me. He was a big boy and wasn't into hugging. Maggs whispered in my ear that she was so happy I was home. I must have cried a liter of tears of joy. It was so good to be home again. I fell asleep with tears of joy in my eyes that night.

A week went by and Dad returned from his hunting trip. At first he was cordial to me and then began asking questions like, "You left because of your mom didn't you?" to which I would say 'no'. It was hard to tell him it was his fault. I still feared his anger.

We received word that the man who beat me up was caught. He had followed my bus from Oregon in a car. He mistook me as the lady who had left him standing at the justice of the peace ten years earlier. He committed a crime which landed him in prison. He was out of prison on parole but was to remain in his county for the duration of his sentence. He not only left the county but crossed the state line following me. He was arrested in a small town in Idaho. He had a hearing and was sentenced to jail. He would then be remanded to the State of Oregon to stand trial for parole violation and to complete his sentence and more. The problem was that when he was left standing at the Justice of the Peace office I was only six years old on a farm in Idaho. I must have been a dead ringer for his girlfriend. This man died in the Idaho State Corrections in the eighties.

After a couple of months at home, it was clear the same old cycle was about to begin as Dad beat me once more for what I considered a very mundane event. My Dad discovered my cousin Carol and I had been singing and dancing in a county bar. We got paid for dancing with the patrons in the bar. It was easy money for us. We both looked much older than we were, so no questions were asked. I never did find out how my father ascertained I was singing and dancing in that bar. He called me horrible names like, whore and slut. I should have been amazed at the ease he called me those things, yet I wasn't. It was as if he could not help himself. Carol and I only danced and sang and nothing more. We only drank ice tea for our beverage.

Dad had contacted the owner and the owner did say we had been there singing but we never did anything wrong. Dad did not believe him, or maybe it was vital that he find another excuse to beat me. It seemed difficult for him to restrain himself from punching someone. The pressure cooker in him needed a safety valve to blow and he pulling off his belt and striking out with it was that explosive release.

The pain from that belt was all too common. Each whip to my backside wrenched through my body yet I refused to make a sound. Sting upon sting curled me into fetal position. Then I heard my brother or sister yell out "Stop it. You are killing her." He stopped for a moment and I was gone running into the grain field. I could not return home that day because I knew Dad would be so angry I would receive another beating.

After dark I began to walk and I ended up several miles from home at the Snake River. The sand was still warm from the sun shining all day. I scooped a little pit in the sand and lay in it and covered myself with the warm sand. I woke early in the morning with a singing seagull flying around in circles above me. I sat up and felt the stabbing in my back. I brushed off some of the sand and it was red. I slipped into the river to clean the sand and blood. It was shockingly cold and woke me into a strong determination to go to Aunt Lizzy's house. I began walking to town when an old, maybe 1930 truck came along and stopped. I looked up at the worn gray wooden side boards and some children and teens were in the back. They were all black. I walked to the passenger side and a wrinkle brown face looked down at me and asked where I was going. She must have been the mother or grandmother of he children in the back of the truck. She agreed to take me to the outskirts of my town. Her smile was infectious and I smiled back.

I felt safe and the children smiled at me. They were cute. A young girl and boy around ages seven to nine made funny faces making me laugh. The truck stopped just outside of town and I got down. I walked for about a mile to my Aunt Lizzy's house. I went to the back door and the morning bottles of milk were there from the daily delivery. I knocked and the door opened.

My aunt looked at me and gasped, "What happened to you? Come in here right now." I picked up the milk bottles and placed them on the table. It was so hard to tell her that dad beat me. But finally she got it out of me.

She ran a tub of hot water with Epson Salts and helped me into the soothing water yet it did sting all over my back. She brought me a large glass of milk. I had been in so much pain I did not realize I was hungry. I watched as she got the Merthiolate out of the medicine cabinet. She left me soaking and said she was going to cook breakfast for me.

I soaked for awhile and then my mother came through the bathroom door. She burst into tears when she saw me. She helped me out of the tub and wrapped me in a towel and then began applying the Merthiolate to the open wounds on my back. Aunt Lizzy opened the band-aid box and began pulling the protective strips off the Band-Aids as mom placed one on each wound. I could hear her sobbing quietly. I ate the bacon and eggs sitting on the table and toast with homemade butter. Mom and Aunt Lizzy talked for awhile and then mom drove me home.

I finally told my mother I would be leaving with a friend for Phoenix. I just could not stick around and be a punching bag for my alcoholic father. For years he had beat mom and now I was added to his list.

Mom hugged me at the bus station and gave me some money to help me until I found a job in Phoenix.

"Please call me often to let me know you are alright" she begged.

"I promise I will, Mom."

My Native American Indian friend Carol, from a town in eastern Idaho and I rode a Greyhound bus to Phoenix. We had high hopes of a new future. She insisted on calling herself an Indian. She had all the features of an Indian and was proud of them. People often asked if they could take her picture which made her feel proud and special.

We both landed a job at a restaurant where young people frequented. It was hard work but I felt a boost of self-esteem. We were able to afford a motel-kitchenette and paid rent by the week. Since I had a social security card in the name of Mae Lovins, I kept that name for the job. I was used to being called Rita. It felt like a comfortable glove that protected me from the scars of my life growing up under the domineering father who treated me like a poor rabid animal.

A pink Cadillac was parked next door. One day I noticed the Cadillac pull up, several girls got out and headed toward the room next door. Then out of the driver's seat emerged a giant black man. He wore gold chains and amulets around his neck. He looked at least seven feet tall and his shoulders seemed to be three feet broad. I was afraid as I had not had much experience with black people other than the ones who gave me a ride to my home town. And once as a child. I was not sure what he was doing. Carol said he looked like a man who owns working girls.

I wondered what that meant. Carol wasted no time explaining the details. I was in awe of her knowledge of so much in life. My fear grew as I envisioned the man abducting me and turning me into one of his girls.

CHAPTER 2

THIRD TRIP TO HEAVEN

**Be not forgetful to entertain
strangers: for thereby some have
entertained angels unawares.
Hebrews 13:2**

We had been working for about two weeks. Carol
stayed and continued to work until they closed.
I road the bus home to our little bungalow (as
we called it) and decided I would take a bath,
eat a bite and go to bed. I was quite tired after
working an extra-long shift on a Saturday night.
The restaurant had a dance floor which attracted
many teens from around the city metro area.
They always had money and drank lots of soft
drinks, ate hot-dogs, fries and hamburgers. I felt
greasy. I lingered in the hot bath. Reluctantly I
got out but the water was getting cold. I found a

partial package of baloney and some mayonnaise in the refrigerator and made a sandwich with wilted browning lettuce. I ate three quarters of the sandwich and put the rest in the refrigerator as it had a funny taste.

Bed was welcomed with a sigh. I fell into a stupor from which I drifted in and out, the bed was spinning and the whole world seemed to be bouncing around in space. I was sick yet I could not get out of bed and I fell into a deep sleep.

A man's voice was saying "You're going to be alright. Just stay with me." Through the fog I could see a big man but who could he be. He looked like the man next door. Was he kidnapping me? I did not care.

I drifted back into softness of nothing. I opened my eyes and I was in a car with fluffy fur engulfing me. The man's Cadillac had white fur on the seats. It was like a white cloud. I faded into oblivion as lights seemed to dance around me. I was in the big man's arms as he pushed through a door and stopped in front of a nurse. She had the whitest dress I had ever seen. I could not hold up my head. His big hand cradled my head ever so gently as if he was protecting a fragile baby bird.

"What do you mean you won't take her?" the man's voice boom.

In a sympathetic voice the nurse said, "This is private hospital. You have to take her to the county hospital. She doesn't look like she has the means to pay for a stay in this hospital."

'What were they talking about?' I thought as the lights all around me cradled me like a new born babe in her mother's arms.

I felt him place me on something hard and turned to the nurse and pulled a roll of money from his pocket, slammed it on the counter and boomed out "You better take care of her and take care of her good! If this isn't enough there is more where this came from, lady! If anything happens to her I will tear this hospital apart with my bare hands."

I slipped into the blackness, yet was it black? The lights continued to surround me in a cozy shell.

I found myself looking down at a curious site. Doctors and nurses were gathered around a bed working on someone. They were trying to revive a girl. "The poor thing", I thought "I hope she is okay." Then I saw the doctor, who had been barking commands, cut the underwear off the girl. I recognized those panties. They were mine. I saw him cut off my panties.

It was an amusing scene and I seemed to float out into the hall and to a room with a six beds. In the corner was a kind old lady. "I am happy you came to visit. I am Grace" she said to me with a sweet smile.

I floated over to her and she told me she was all alone and she only saw a nurse once in a while. She had been so lonely but felt better now that I had come to visit with her. She told me about how her husband would talk to her even though he was already dead.

I began to float away and she said, "Please don't leave me."

I said, 'I will come back and visit you soon". She seemed to be content with my answer. I had no idea why I said that to her.

Out the door I went and found myself soaring up away from the city and all I could see was a bright light of pure love and peace beckoning me. I was so happy that I sort of swayed back and forth with a bit of dancing swirl like a music box dancer. I wanted to be with that light in a most desperate way. I wanted to travel faster. The Light was brighter than anything I had ever witnessed: as if a trillion, billion sparklers were ignited at the same time with a glow that lit up the entire universe.

I saw people hovering in place and some floating slower and some faster than I was, as I continued my transit across the beautiful void that seemed to go on forever as an endless echo. As I came closer to the light I encountered people who knew me and I seemed to know them. Love emanated from them and from all around me but mostly from the beautiful Light. I encountered beings who I knew were kindred to me yet I had never known them on the shadow side of the veil or earth plain. Many were my ancient relatives. We all seemed to be dancing around with joy. My great-grandmother came to me with a loving glow of what I can only describe as a hug. I have never met her as she was born in 1855 and died in 1930 before I was born in 1945. I knew instantly that Great Grandmother was my guardian angel, and helper. She was my mother's grandmother. It all seemed so natural. I knew I had been here before. It felt so familiar as if I had come back home. I found Bernie again or did she find me? She smiled and stayed with me as if to just keep me company.

I realize my point of view may be different from someone else. What I saw and experienced may not quite appear the way someone else would see things. We are all different. We all have our own points of reference and we see things from that point of view. There are many people who have near death experiences and they may differ from my experience. We are all one with the One Source yet we are like individual snowflakes as we are all different. Each is a part of Source-God observing all from a different point of view.

CHAPTER 3

HEAVEN IS REAL

I found myself in a beautiful garden and orchard
with colors so vivid and aromas so beautiful
that I wanted to bathe there forever in that bliss.
In the center of the orchard was someone in
white with white light flowing easily from and
around him or her like a white sari. The lovely
angelic being seemed to be the teacher. I sat on
a white bench like the white marble benches
I had seen in pictures of old Greece with the
Greek philosopher, Socrates of long ago. But
the bench was soft and velvety not the hard
marble I would have expected. Soon I was in
a group and they accepted me as one of them.
The lessons I learned were heartwarming and
filled me with joy.

The colors were so vivid that they made the
colors on earth seem as if they were black and

white. The sweetest music filled the eternal space and the aromas were of every flower and yet more. They were so wonderful and I could distinguish each individual aroma from the total array.

At first it seemed I was receiving information slowly then as time passed the speed of the incoming knowledge was easy to absorb.

Out of nowhere more heavenly beings began to appear around the teacher. They were familiar in an unfamiliar way. They were teachers who had come to earth to help us understand what our purpose is and why we are here. They have been coming to earth from before known history. They had been in many lands and today there are a few back on earth at this time to help us move forward in our levels of evolution until we too become one who may want to come to earth to teach others. I knew Jesus, Mohammad, Abraham, a few teachers from Buddhism and Hinduism to name only a few. Some were getting ready to come to earth for another life time to help point mankind in the right direction. Some were women and some men. It did not seem to matter the gender one would incarnate to help us. The only thing that mattered was the message and lessons of Love, Forgiveness, Thanksgiving, and with all these comes perfect Joy. Some call it Bliss. Those who have reached that level of evolution of being in the Bliss or forever in the heaven rhelm need not return to continue learning and observing. But they may chose to come back for all of us out of pure Love. I did learn that many who had come before to help us advance in our evolution toward Bliss are called saints. Some are called great teachers and Gurus. The direction seemed so simple. If one is facing our origins in God then we are on our path but if we are facing away from God we are not on our path and life is not the way it was planned.

I felt the message tell me I would understand this more as I grew older. I did not realize at that point I would not be allowed to remain in the heaven realm.

We are all children of the same Universe. It seemed so many religions were represented and I knew all were one. It is difficult to describe the meaning of this but it is true. I saw teachers representing so many such as <u>Judaism</u>, <u>Christianity</u>, <u>Islam</u>, <u>Baha'i</u>, <u>Hinduism</u>, <u>Taoism</u>, <u>Buddhism</u>, <u>Sikhism</u>, <u>Rodnoveri</u>, <u>Celtic</u>, <u>Pagan</u>, <u>Heathenism</u>, <u>Semitic pagan</u>, <u>Wicca</u>, <u>Kemetism</u>, <u>Hellenismos</u>, <u>Roman pagan</u> and many more that have been lost over the centuries. Here they became all one with us all. We are each on our own level of development and they know this is good. I smiled as I watched all of them having a great time laughing and talking. Some were even telling cute jokes. It seemed that being in the Heaven realm is joyous and happy and peoples' happy spirits show it.

I understood Jesus travelled through the far and middle East in his younger years starting around the age of 16 to learn from teachers in India and China during his life on the earth. He began his journey in Egypt. It was not until the end of his life on earth did he settle in the Near East.

I saw what looked something like fluffy clouds or cocoons floating in the distance with many ministering beings carefully speaking and stroking the cocoons. It reminded me of the care given to premature babies in an intensive care unit. There were many different shades of dark gray to light pink and a few almost white. I wondered what the darkest one was.

"That is Hitler." The message popped into my being, "He has not been able to understand that he was not the savior of mankind. He also experiences guilt as he is a part of God yet he does not realize that fact. Until he comes to the realization that Love is the only answer and he is part of the whole, he will remain in his isolation of self-pity. It may take millions of years before he realizes he is part of the whole".

I gasped. This is why it is better to forgive and be forgiven on earth. Then I experienced the thoughts "It is necessary that we forgive ourselves". I have many things in my life for which I am not proud. I have learned that it is past and I now forgive myself. I forgive any who have hurt me and who have compelled and manipulated me to do things that are not right. The actions and attitude we have here will be reflected when we cross over. We become our own judge from our Higher Self of Being and that being is with God and is God. Some of the cocoons were older than Hitler and others were since his crossing.

The message made me a little sad. I knew I must send loving thoughts to those in the cocoons so they could come out and join us in this All Encompassing Love and see that Love is ALL. I learned beautiful ways to pray for and meditate for everyone. For each act of Love toward another I receive the joyful Love back many times over.

Love is the All. Love is the Healer. Love is Forgiveness. Love is God.

I know that I can try as I might to convince someone of a particular reasoning or religion but I cannot change that person.

That change comes from within the person. If one feels they have the only answer to gaining access to heaven, it only means that person has not evolved or progressed past that point in life. Life on Earth can be thought of as a class room and the more lessons we learn the more we progress. It is OK to be on this level right where you are. It will benefit the person when the realization is finally discovered that the truth of God is much more than one religion or belief system. A person may be on the correct path to Bliss and this could be the last incarnation on the earth side. Just as we start out in preschool as little children we progress through the grades. Some go on to collage. Others move on the masters and doctorate degrees. Some find themselves studying more subjects and progress with more degrees. On earth we consider them scholarly. The progress of our own evolution is similar to the education of earth.

I learned more about the need to be forgiving and loving on the earth side of life. For many centuries than we know, many souls or spirits were born of the earth to bring lessons to us in a powerful way. Many were rejected as heretics. In the future, many will choose to be born to do the same. Others choose to be born to learn lessons and to further spirit growth to the ultimate level back to Source. I got the impression our prayers for souls who have crossed over may help lighten the cocoon and bring them closer to joining the rest in the heaven realm in the Bliss.

I wondered about the people who were moving at different speeds as I was soaring to the Light. The answer came to me without the need to ask. The ones traveling very slowly or not moving were having trouble vacating the physical body. Some were lingering in severe illness. Others were being held back artificially with machines attached to their body to keep the body functioning. I wondered why they had to linger like that and sure enough the answer popped into my being. People around the dead person were trying to keep the person alive. They did not want the loved one to leave. The person who was trying to cross over, was sad because he or she was being held back. They wanted to go to the light just like the rest of us who have crossed over. This begs the question: Should we keep someone on life-support who has lived a long life or who has very little chance of being a vibrant human again? Are we torturing that person for our own selfish needs or are we fearful of death ourselves? Saying good-byes to the person and letting them go is a Loving act. If that person still remains after being taken off life-support for a time then they are following their path. I do believe recitation efforts should be started if someone dies but not if the person is elderly and has lived a long life. There are several religious groups that have opinions on the subject. You may learn more about end of life on the internet

To my surprise and joy I met my helpers from the heaven plane. They were around my great-grandmother. I was filled with utter elation to be with them again. When we are born, all memory of the past lives is gone. We suddenly have amnesia of our past. I began to remember I had lived many past lives on earth and other realms. In this life I wanted to learn to forgive and to help others learn to love and to forgive. Others in my group stepped up and volunteered to help me. My mother wanted to learn certain lessons and accomplish more of her life plan and my father stepped forward to learn tolerance, and enlightenment. Everyone hopes they will be able to heed the prompting of their helpers to reach their goal and some choose a role to accomplish something or many things to expand their understanding behind the veil of the heavenly plain. Some help us fulfill our goal by being what is considered a bad person in the earth plane while all the while they are only fulfilling the desire of the spirit or soul. Not all who hurt us or cause us pain, are on the wrong path. Some may go farther than planned in that state because they are not listening to the promptings for the helpers.

I learned my goal was to bring truth and love to everyone I could possibly reach. I am to help erase the fear of death. I was humbled when I realized what my goal was. I am also to spread the word of Life not Death. All is Life. When we step through the door of death we are actually back home in the Heaven Realm with all of our loved ones. I then realized that is partly why my father was brutal to me. Whatever I did following the harshness of my father propelled me to the next step in my life. Some realize they have overdone their part when they become addicted to alcohol, gambling or drugs and even food. This may alter their roll to help one live the life wanted but help is still there. The reason I mention this is because my father became an alcoholic. When he would come home drunk he was mean and would very often strike out at someone, mainly my mother. Other times it would be me and my brothers and sister. It is possible he went too far into the roll of being the brute that guided others lives.

CHAPTER 4

REINCARNATION

This has been taken directly from REINCARNATION IN THE NEW TESTAMENT http://reincarnation.ws/reincarnation_in_the _new_testament.html

THE BLIND MAN

As he went along, he saw a man blind from birth. His disciples asked him, "Rabbi, who sinned, this man or his parents, that he was born blind?" John 9:1-2, NIV

The disciples wanted to know the reason for the man's blindness. They offered two possibilities to Jesus. Either the man was blind because of the sins of his parents or he was blind because he was reaping the fruit of his own sins (karma). If our souls do not exist prior to this birth and if the man was born blind, then when or where could he have committed the sins that caused his blindness? His soul would have existed prior to that birth and he would have been engaged in a corporeal setting with other people to commit sins against or with. In other words, the blind man had a previous life. This indicates that the per-existence of the soul was a prevalent idea among the disciples, otherwise how could they have asked such an unusual question? Neither does Jesus ask them where they got such a strange idea. He does not marvel that they have presented him with such a foolish concept. Where did they get this idea? As we have seen in the "blind man" scripture and other scriptures, the concept of reincarnation was understood by Jesus and the disciples. They employed the concept in these discussions in a matter-of-fact way.

ELIJAH'S RETURN

Elijah the prophet is believed to have lived in the ninth century B.C.E. At the point of his death a fiery chariot with horses of fire took him in a whirlwind to heaven and he was seen no more (II Kings 2:11). Four hundred years later, Malachi closed the last lines of the Old Testament with a prophecy from God stating that God would send Elijah before the "great and terrible day of the Lord" comes (Malachi 4:5). The Jewish people were expecting Elijah to return as the necessary preface to signal the coming of the Messiah.

The disciples all felt that Jesus was the Messiah but they were puzzled. Where is Elijah? The disciples asked the Master about this and he told them that Elijah had already returned as John the Baptist. The first discussion of this is in Matthew, chapter 11.

I tell you the truth: Among those born of women there has not risen anyone greater than John the Baptist; yet he who is least in the kingdom of heaven is greater than he. From the days of John the Baptist until now, the kingdom of heaven has been forcefully advancing, and forceful men lay hold of it. For all the Prophets and the Law prophesied until John. And if you are willing to accept it, he is the Elijah who was to come. He who has ears, let him hear. Matthew 11:11-15, NIV

The disciples asked him, "Why then do the teachers of the law say that Elijah must come first?" Jesus replied, "To be sure, Elijah comes and will restore all things. But I tell you, Elijah has already come, and they did not recognize him, but have done to him everything they wished. In the same way the Son of Man is going to suffer at their hands." Then the disciples understood that he was talking to them about John the Baptist. Matthew 17:10-13, NIV

The above scripture indicates that the disciples and Jesus believed in reincarnation. John the Baptist was the reincarnation of Elijah. In an attempt to fit these scriptures into the orthodox view of one-life-only, some believe that Elijah never died as we know it because he went up in a chariot of fire, thus discounting John the Baptist as an instance of reincarnation. Their thinking is that Elijah did inhabit John the Baptist but it was not rebirth because Elijah had never died. For this "discounting" to really work, the Baptist would need to have returned in the same fiery chariot as a grown man. However, he was clearly placed in the womb of a human mother after which he had a very mortal and common birth. Jesus said he was "born of woman" and in Luke 1:13-17, an angel tells John's father, Zacharias, that John will be born to his wife Elizabeth... "And he will go before him in the spirit and power of Elijah." Others use this last line to say that John the Baptist was under the power of Elijah but was not the incarnation of Elijah. However, Jesus says in no uncertain terms that John is Elijah and not simply an ambassador of Elijah's power, "This is Elijah... He who has ears to hear let him hear" (Matthew 11:14-15). Also, Malachi does not say that Elijah will appear by proxy but that Elijah himself will return.

WHO IS THE SON OF MAN?

Yet another discussion between Jesus and the disciples underscores their belief in reincarnation.

When Jesus came to the region of Caesarea Philippi, he asked his disciples, "Who do people say the Son of Man is?" They replied, "Some say John the Baptist; others say Elijah; and still others, Jeremiah or one of the prophets." "But what about you?" he asked. "Who do you say I am?" Simon Peter answered, "You are the Christ, the Son of the living God." Matthew 16:15-16

The flow here seems to be that if a prophet were to appear he must be the incarnation of one of the prophets from the past and so Jesus is asking the disciples who the people think has incarnated as Jesus. The idea of the reincarnation of the prophets is taken for granted and the sole point of the question is to find out who the multitudes believe him to be. These scriptures indicate that, at least to Jesus and the disciples, the concept of reincarnation was common fare. Herod also heard that others were saying one of the prophets of long ago had reincarnated. This again indicates that such a belief in reincarnation was common at that time.

Now Herod the tetrarch heard about all that was going on. And he was perplexed, because some were saying that John had been raised from the dead, others that Elijah had appeared, and still others that one of the prophets of long ago had come back to life. Luke 9:7-8, NIV This information was found at: Reincarnation in bible http://reincarnation. ws/reincarnation_in_the_new_testament.html

While I was on the Heaven side of the veil, I remembered some of my past lives. In my most previous life I had harbored hate for people and wanted to do them harm. Now I wanted to learn to forgive everyone, including myself. But I had not done this. It seemed a very difficult task while living on earth. Here I was beyond the veil and my life plan had not been accomplished. Was I going to plan it all over again and find new parents to bring me into the earth plane? I felt I would just remain in heaven as I hovered there soaking up all the beautiful knowledge. Who knew I would be sent back to complete my missions?

I realized the black man who rescued me was a kind man. His life on earth was to be the helper of the girls he took around town to earn money in the way they had chosen for this life time. He protected them from harm. He was my angel unaware.

My previous life I was a man who was intolerant of other races and life styles. It was during the civil war and I just knew I was fighting on the right side to keep slavery alive. I killed many from the north with joy. I bragged about the number of men I had killed at the end of each day. When the war was over I was angry at the northerners and I cheered when I learned President Lincoln was killed. I died a lonely broken man who was homeless and without any friends. No one wanted to be around a bitter vengeful man.

Then I felt beings around me with the same feelings they were working on to overcome. They wanted to enter the earth plane to work on their past life hatred of others and to learn forgiveness and love. In a way this made me feel better because I knew I was not the only one. We do carry many of our emotions with us to the other side. When we die here and cross over with our baggage. The incarnations on a planet is our time to learn to Love and forgive on the deepest level possible.

Some of our incarnations are not on the earth plane. There are so many other planes of existence that the earth is only a minute particle of the whole. On earth we are carbon units. On others we are made of other substances. There are other dimensions or parallel life existences we can join on our journey back to the Love, Source, God. Many of these can be found by doing research on your own.

It seemed hazy about the rest of the plans I had made before I was born in Idaho in nineteen forty five (1945). I tried to see but it was fuzzy. Then I remembered another life time my father sold me to a family as a slave worker to a French family. I had a daughter by the man of the house. It felt like it was in the fifteen hundred's (1500's): time does not have meaning across the veil. My daughter was never allowed to play outside. As she grew she had to remain in the little room at the top of the house as I cleaned and cooked all day for the family. I knew the only life she would be allowed to live would be as a prostitute or a worker for another family just as I was. She pined to play outside as she watched the daughter and son of my master play in the beautiful courtyard below. A beautiful hanging garden filled half of the courtyard where the children played together. My daughter begged me to let her go down and play. I became so sad thinking of the life that lies ahead of her and I devised a plan. The master would not allow me to bring her out of the little room. I often played with her at night. She especially enjoyed the game of blind fold and finding objects in the room. I placed the blindfold on her and I picked her up and opened the shutters on the one window of the room. I then stepped out on the loose terracotta roof tiles. The tiles slipped as I expected and we began to fall three stories down and we were thrust to the other side of the veil. We were in the Loving Light together.

Years later in 1973, my daughter was three years old; she surprised me while we were playing a game. "Mommy, I am happy you played that game with me where we jumped off the house and we died. I didn't want to live like that again. All I wanted to do was play with the little children."

I questioned her, "What are you talking about honey?"

She looked at me with her impish smile, "You know! When you put the blind fold on me and picked me up and took me out the window and stepped on that red brick roof."

Time seemed to stop as I realized what she had just said. She remembered the previous life so long ago and I realized that little girl was my daughter again. Now I wondered how many times we had been together in other lifetimes. I did learn children remember parts of previous lives, even the Heaven realm when they are born and up until they are around 3 or 4 years old. Often those comments they make are stifled by adults as silly imaginations.

In another life-time I saw myself as a Native American Indian man running from a strange two headed animal. It had a shiny head and a head of a strange beast. The beast was waving a shiny curved tooth back and forth with an extra appendage and it was bearing down on me fast. The two headed beast was the most frighting animal I had ever seen. Clouds of dust billowed behind it as it came closer at a speed I could never run. It was the fiercest animal I had ever encountered. I knew the two headed animal would kill me. I was running and looked down and saw leather leggings and moccasins. My leggings were greasy from many years of wiping my hands on them after eating and killing food. I stopped short at a roaring river. If I jumped in I would surly die and if I did not the animal would kill me. Just then the animal was upon me and the huge shiny tooth swooped down and cut my back open and I fell into the river. I gasped for air as the river carried me away tumbling in the torrent. 'Ah!' I was in the Light. There was no pain in the crossing over. I looked down and saw a conquistador reigning in his horse as he watched the bobbing figure in the river as swirls of crimson surrounded the Native Indian of Mexico. In my current life I was born with a birth mark on my back of many freckles in a half moon shape where the conquistador had slashed open my back. Now I know we often carry marks and attitudes from a past life forward. Many generations of guilt or love can be building, depending on the past lives.

In this life I can focus on Forgiveness, Love for All, and Joy. Again! Each morning I awaken and say 'Thank You' to that Power, God that envelops me and holds me so close. This is one of the lessons I learned from Wayne Dyer. I appreciate his writings as they have helped me and many others step even closer to enlightenment.

Watching the teacher, I was fascinated by the glow of golden-white light that emanated around him or was it female. I could not tell. The light pulsed out, then back in a rhythmic flow resembling the shape of a heart. The type of heart I would draw for Valentine's Day. Could this be why angels were painted with wings? Had others experienced what I was seeing and gone back to live on Earth to tell about it? Could some of the artists of old have experienced crossing over?

I absorbed the knowledge at a remarkable rate. I began to understand that on earth I believed that God was outside of me; I was separate from God. I was filled with guilt because I was born a sinner. Now I began to realize that we are all an interconnected whole, and separation is an illusion. Time and space are illusions. I am not only connected to God I am an aspect of God. As an aspect of God I am experiencing things from many points of view. I am learning each step of the way to become fully One-With-God again. I am now learning that everything is part of this whole, the universe, stars, space, worlds, planets, people, animals and all living and non-living. All is motion, energy and thought. It is like a drop of water in the ocean is part of the whole and the ocean is part of the drop.

Another example is to realize that a little corpuscle in your little toe is part of you and you are part of that corpuscle. Each part of our body is necessary to keep the whole body functioning. We can lose some parts of our body and continue functioning. My arm is part of my body and my body is part of my arm. Only a few things if lost would cause us to stop this body from living such as loss of my heart, liver, kidneys or brain. What if my body is a small part of our solar system? I then would be part of our solar system and solar system would be part of me and you. We can take this further and say our solar system is a part of our galaxy and our galaxy is part of the solar system. Now we can move on to include all that is until we come to the infinity of Source, Divine Light, God. All is part of God and God is part of all. We have heard the term that we are made of star dust. These words are true but they are only part of the truth. To learn more I recommend you look up Quantum Physics. There is an abundance of information available to the lay person. "Quantum" comes from the Latin meaning "how much." It refers to the discrete units of matter and energy that are predicted by and observed in quantum physics. Even space and time, which appear to be extremely continuous, have smallest possible values.

Physical reality is made up from energy manifest to allow us to experience all that we can as part of God. The curiosity of God wants to experience all aspects of what can and is. All that we experience is part of our plan. Sometimes what we plan and what becomes fact may change. At this point our helpers try to nudge us to the right direction.

That gut-feeling or intuition, ever so subtle, is trying to prompt us to follow the right course as planned. These feelings are our guides working with us. When we follow our guide's promptings our life seems to be magical. We call many of these experiences miracles. When we do something and later say 'I wish I had paid attention to my intuition. I would have been OK, if I had gone that direction'. Even to this day I sometimes fail to respond to my intuition and I feel a pang of guilt because I know better.

Guilt is another aspect we learn on the Earth side. We learn guilt from our parents, teachers, and religious leaders and in general most adults. We heard, 'You should not do that! Don't do that again!' and the list goes on. One lesson to learn is to 'Love Myself'. If I cannot love myself, I cannot truly love others and love all things? In my present life I was taught that I was born a sinner and needed to be baptized to get into heaven. If I was not baptized I would go to a place like heaven but I would not see God. I also went to catechism to learn how sinful I was and I had to go to confession in a confessional at least every week to be forgiven for my sins so I could get into heaven. I learned heaven was going to be a very difficult goal to reach. I would be lucky to make it to Purgatory. Purgatory, according to Catholic Church doctrine, is an intermediary state after physical death in which those destined for Heaven "undergo purification, so as to achieve the holiness necessary to enter the joy of heaven".

Only those who die in the state of grace but have not in life reached a sufficient level of holiness can be in Purgatory, and therefore no one in Purgatory will remain forever in that state or go to hell. This theological notion has ancient roots and is well-attested in early Christian literature, but the poetic conception of Purgatory as a geographically existing place is largely the creation of medieval Christian piety and imagination.

I believe this concept came into reality when one or more were considered very pious gave their explanation of what they encountered when they too had a NDE. Had some seen the cocoons or dense clouds as I did? It is possible and it was used by the church to help people understand they should do good works. I believe much of the narrations of those who returned was not kept or written down. It could have been deleted. We do not know what was in the minds of the people recording what anyone would have reported about being on the other side. Scribes in one year may copy text onto tablets or parchment and 100 years later more scribes would copy those parchments. Parts of the pages could have broken off and the scribe filled in with what he felt should be in that empty space. Another 100 years the pages would be copied again. With each century passing more changes would be made. The Vatican has libraries with so many scriptures it makes me wonder which is correct and how many could be read and brought back to the original. We can read ancient scripts from the east and Far East and find similar stories to the ones we find in the newer scriptures. There are people today translating those ancient scripts so that more knowledge will be made available to those who desire to learn. I am one of those who want to read all of the Sanskrit and learn the ancient knowledge that Jesus learned on his travels from about age 17 to 30 when he returned to the Holy Land. Oh! Didn't I mention that before? Jesus did spend his early years travelling and learning from the masters in the East. If you are doubtful of such a concept, remember that kings or wise men came from the East after his birth bearing gifts.

CHAPTER 5

LESSONS ABOUT LIFE

God is experiencing life through us. We also come into this realm to be an observer.

Lessons about same sex attractions: First I will ask a question for those who believe anyone born with the desire to be with someone of the same gender exists and why they cannot change that reality.

"Why would anyone want to be a person that is attracted to someone of the same gender? Why would someone subject themselves to ridicule and bullying? Why would someone want to live where others would have such hate they would torture and or kill him or her?" The answers are many but please be sure of one thing. Lesbian, *gay*, bisexual and transgender (LGBT) are real. No one can turn someone from one to another. We are all born the way we are whether LGBT or so-called straight. They are not pretending and no one learns to be gay (LGBT). It just is. I do hope you realize this while you read on. I hope you are not prejudiced.

Now is the time to learn Love and Tolerance. I had to do it. I am so happy I have this time to correct those miss-concepts that I had in past lives. In the past when a boy was born with no testicles or non-descending testicles the doctor would advise the parents to allow the penis to be removed. It was felt before the 1940's that the person would grow up happier as a girl. All they had to do was treat the person as a girl in every way and he would be a girl. The problem was it did not work. That girl grew up attracted to girls. This is proof you cannot change a person's gender preference.

I was witness to many spirits making plans to return to earth soon. Each individual who would arrive on the earth with same gender love: some offered to be the daughter or son of someone who wanted to learn to love and rid them of bigotry. One was incarnated too many times as a female and planned to be male in this next life. He would be male in his new life but the female character had been imprinted so long on his previous lives he would like males just as if he was still a female. Another wanted to learn forgiveness for being female in a male body that retained the traits of a female within and learn to be happy with self as is. Another volunteered to be his father because he wanted to learn tolerance as he had been bigoted in previous life times. This scenario is very common. He wanted to love his son unconditionally. Helpers agreed to help the father through his goal. Another was to be born into the earth side who wanted to learn tolerance and unconditional love. Another would soon be born as a boy and be in love with other boys, men in love with men and women in love with women. They know from a very early age in childhood they are different from what society says is normal in this day and time. When they hear stories of hatred toward others like themselves, they learn guilt and fear at a young age. By doing so he would help the man learn unconditional love by accepting his son. This answers the age-old question, 'why is someone gay? Why can they not just learn to love someone of the opposite gender?' It is their life path. Many are here to teach us to love unconditionally. Have I learned that lesson? I have never considered the LGBT differently in my present lifetime. I have always loved them unconditionally. My late husband did not at first but later accepted them as normal. Many are here to learn to love. We are all the same regardless of gender preference. We are all a part of the Divine, the Origin, the Source: God.

We all worked in our own group to plan our life. Our life can change as we move forward. It depends on ones willingness to learn. The first lesson is to remember what we dwell on is what happens to us. I will go into this more later. In fact, one of my goals was to help many who struggle with the stigma of hatred from family who are manifesting as LGBT.

I was struck by the fact that The Light Is. The Light Is God in every religion going back as far as the beginning: Creator, Source. Light is Love. Light and Love equals God. We all have the spark of light within each of us both in our physical body and our spirit body. The Light pulsates as our heart pulses. This rhythm is in everything as is light (pure energy). There is no such thing as true darkness: only Dark Matter (Dark Matter is simply in another spectrum that we cannot see with our eyes.). Then, the teacher allowed the knowledge that the Light is the Breath of God or Infinite Source.

> *Again Jesus spoke to them, saying, "I am the light of the world. Whoever follows me will not walk in darkness, but will have the light of life." John 8:12*

I Am. I Am that I Am. Those words have special meaning for us. Jesus spoke many times about being our brother. He became incarnated on earth to help people understand that we are not separate from God and we are all one with all. Much of the translation was lost through the centuries. Human error is always a given when texts are copied over and over again and from one language to another. Throughout time many words and meanings change. I learned that some of the translations were done by scribes who were given a specific agenda to write scripture in such a way as to benefit those in power at different moments in time. Some scriptures were adopted from far older Sanskrit from the East. If I had a physical body my mouth would have dropped open in astonishment.

I learned that a woman was born in 1910 in the Middle East. She was now in India helping many people. She helped the poorest of the poor and never turned anyone away. She incarnated to help and to teach us to Love God and of the LOVE Of GOD. I had not heard of her but I knew while I was in the presence of the angelic teacher that she would become famous one day and she would die quietly. She is one of the Spirits that did not need to incarnate on earth but chose this life. Later I learned she served the poorest of the poor in Calcutta. I met a beautiful spirit who had been on the heaven side for awhile and she was part of the little nun's plan. She would be famous and have 2 sons who would be the most famous in the world from the time of their birth to their death. She agreed to die and cross over into heaven just a little while before nun does so the spirit of Mother Teresa will not be in the news day after day. She simply wanted to pass back without fanfare. Through my own research I find that that person must have been Princess Diana. Princess Diana died August 31, 1997 and Mother Teresa died September 5, 1997. The circumstances of the Princess' death were in the news for months that followed. The nun from Calcutta died five days after the Princess. Thus she received about five days of international news. This is the plan. They both had an interest in helping with HIV/AIDS. I felt a compelling need to help with that affliction that would arrive several years later, even though I had no idea how I would help.

I have been criticized for my love of Mother Teresa by some people. Some claim she should never have turned everyone into a Christian in an Indian Country. They should have been taught the Hindu way.

I have studied Mother Teresa and I learned from Wikipedia/: Those brought to her home received medical attention and were afforded the opportunity to die with dignity, according to the rituals of their faith; Muslims were read the Qumran, Hindus received water from the Ganges, and Catholics received the Last Rites. "A beautiful death," she said, "is for people who lived like animals to die like angels—loved and wanted. She is one who came to teach us but so many do not listen. This happens all too often when an advanced spirit comes to bring the simple message to us. Another who needs a mention is Mohandas Karamchand Gandhi. My conclusion is that even the well thought of teachers in our present time can make mistakes. We are human in this human body. I hold no grudges for anyone who argues with me. I know we are all at our own level of development and we have much to learn.

In the nineties, I joined Public Health, as one of the HIV Nurses. I worked there for six years. I enjoyed what I did and I was there when many died. It was humbling to help families realize where their loved one was going and the person living with HIV would relax and smile when I explained what they would find as they crossed over.

CHAPTER 6

BACK IN MY BODY

Someone appeared beside me. He seemed to remind me of an angel or maybe Mary or it could have been a Master or even Jesus? It was as if it did not matter who was bringing the message. "It is not your time to be here. You can go back or you can stay. It is up to you. You do have more to do on the earth plain."

Most of what you have learned here will come to you many years later when you are older. Many were hovering around me with love. Some I recognized such as Jesus, Krishna, Mary Magdalene, Elijah, Enoch, Buddha, Michael the messenger or Angel, Angel Uriel who seemed to be my guardian along with my great grandmother. The love around me was beyond my ability to describe on this page. There is no judgment or criticism. Only total love.

I wanted to stay in the total heavenly bliss. Why would I ever want to go back and live in the hardships of earth? This is the most beautiful place to be and I know now I will always have a place here because this is home. But then: I thought, "My mother will cry if I die".

'Poof!' In that instant I felt my spirit ram back into my body. I felt it jolt; it had come back in through the top of my head like the end of a tall telephone poll ramming down into my body.

I was wracked with pain in my chest and throat. I felt my body jerk violently from the reentry of my spirit. Something was over my face and I felt as if my breath was being stifled. A plug was in my throat. I reached up and grabbed a tube and pulled it out of my throat which seemed to scrape my throat like sand paper. I sat up and tried to yell. All that came from my vocal cords was a weak "Ah".

Then I saw the sheet that had shrouded me. Simultaneously I heard a woman scream and the clatter of medal hitting hard surfaces and something stabbed between my legs and quivered. I saw a nurse running out a door; her scream became faint as she distanced herself from where I sat with a dangling flexible hose in my hand. I removed what I later learned was a scalpel between my legs stuck into the thin mattress. I looked down at my chest and red burn marks were pronounced. 'Had I been beaten up? Why was I naked?' I was in so much pain.

I lay back down with a groan as people came into the room and surrounded me. They seemed to scurry every which way like rats disturbed in an abandoned warehouse. Chaos was the rule of the moment. A man began asking me questions like 'what is your name?', 'do you know where you are?' and the questions went on. The room seemed to spin and I was sinking as the room and the people began to fade.

I woke and found I was being wheeled out of the emergency room and down the hall to a room. A bottle dangled above my head and a rubber tube tailed down to my arm. The nurses pushed me into an empty spot and I rasped "No. Go through that door." I pointed vigorously.

A nurse said "this is your assigned room. We are putting you here" she announced in her matter of fact voice.

"No! Go there!" Emphatically I pointed at the other door. My throat was raw and it was painful to talk. "I want to go to Grace. Put me by Grace!" trying to use the most forceful stern voice I could muster. Oh! That hurt! I hoped I would not have to talk again for a long time.

"Who told you Grace was here?" one of the nurses asked.

The nurse who seemed to be in charge said "Okay! We will take you to the next room. We really need you close to the nurses' station.

Finally! There she was in the corner all alone just as I had left her when I promised I would come back and visit. Grace was asleep. I was thankful. I did not need to talk anymore. The nurses were muttering something about how could this girl know of this little old lady whom no one ever visited.

"OK Rita, here is Grace." The woman in white said. She seemed exasperated and ready to just leave the room.

An intravenous needle was in my arm and a nurse put up a new bottle of something clear. It looked like water. Wracked with pain I now found myself in extreme nausea and was unable to hold up my head and I turned to my side and wretched violently. I had no control over my bodily functions. The nurses would come in and clean me and the bed only to have to return in a short time to repeat the process. I think two days past while I traveled wave after wave of absolute sickness. Oh how I wished I was back with the angels and my heavenly tribe-family group. I don't know how many are in one's tribe but it is much more than a thousand. Oh much more! I tried to 'Will' my way back to heaven. I begged God to take me back.

Ah! That was the moment I began to remember what had happened. I heard a man say food poisoning and something like she was dead over 20 minutes. My mind faded in and out of understanding when finally about the fourth day I opened my eyes to the luxurious feeling of warmth on my face. A nurse had draped a hot wash cloth on my face. I reached up and held it to my face inhaling the steam. It felt almost as good as when my mom would rub strong smelling Ben-gay on my chest front and back then place a hot old diaper over my front and back. When we had a cold this was the treatment of choice. I would sleep like a baby. I let it lie there until it became cool.

"Welcome back to the living," a kind female voice said. "We didn't know if you would pull through a second time."

I asked the nurse, "A second time? What happened?"

She said, "You came in and died. We worked on you for a long time and then the doctor said you were dead. Around ten or fifteen minutes later you sat up and scared the nurse so much she had to take a few days off. You were legally dead for more twenty minutes in all. Then two days ago you had to be brought back again." Her eyes were kind. "You came close a few times the first two days. You will be OK now. Just rest! Are you hungry?"

"Yes! I would like some food. May I have some spuds and roast beef?" My mouth was ready for food and my stomach agreed with gurgles.

Laughing, the nurse said, "Not so fast little lady. You will get some gelatin for now. What flavors do you like strawberry or orange?"

Soon I was barraged with many men and women dressed in white lab coats who followed a doctor. He told them about my death and two kinds of food poisoning. I did not understand the names of the bacteria or germs. He asked them questions I did not understand. Some answered with words that meant nothing to me. I do know the doctor in charge described the length of time they tried to revive me after I expired, and then the ten minutes of death plus over ten minutes after they stopped trying to revive me. He said when they name the time of death it is usually longer than the records show because the nurse begins the time at the beginning of the resuscitation. Wow! So I was dead even longer than twenty minutes.

Then he told each one to put on a glove and do a vaginal exam on me. I was startled and did not know what to do. "What are you doing to me? Stop it!" I said with tears in my eyes and they trickled down to my mouth with a salty taste.

The doctor said, "These these are medical students. They need to learn. They will examine all the patients in this hospital. There are medical students in all the hospitals in our cities." His voice had no compassion or tenderness. He sounded like my father who barked orders as if to say, 'this is just the way it is'.

When they had finished, they left me alone. Grace woke and said "I always pretend to be asleep when they come. They don't bother with me anymore". The twinkle in her eyes made me feel better.

"I will remember that when they come in again." We continued to talk and she seemed to perk up more. She looked very old, older than both my grandmothers. I was happy to be in her company.

The nurse brought a tray to me and put the head of my bed up. On the tray was a square of orange gelatin, a cup of broth and two soda crackers. She then put a tray in front of Sarah and began feeding her different colors of what looked like paste.

"Grace. Can't you feed yourself? You must really be old," I chimed in my young naive innocence.

The nurse looked at me and said, "She can't understand what you say and she can't talk".

"We talk all the time. She talks to me," I retorted.

Grace smiled at me and her eyes twinkled. The nurse looked at me like I was a child and said, "Oh honey, it is your imagination. Grace has not been able to talk for a couple of years. She had a stroke."

"But we talk all the time. She hears you talking to her and she knows what you are saying. I guess you just can't hear her. She is a sweet lady even if she is really old." I sipped the broth giving the signal I was unwilling to talk about it anymore. I thought 'that stupid nurse doesn't know what she is talking about'.

The next day I heard a group of people coming to my building so I pretended to be sleeping. I heard them come to my bedside and a large hand shook my shoulder. Startled, I opened my eyes. "A new group of medical students are here today. We need to examine you."

I watched as the men and a woman began putting gloves on and gathered around my bed. Then I saw the woman with long fingernails. The glove looked like it was stretched over a Sikh dagger. She came to the side of the bed and I sat up and yelled, "No you don't. You're not sticking that fingernail in me!"

The commanding doctor put his hand on my shoulder attempting to push me back down on the bed and said, "I told you! This is a teaching hospital and all patients here are examined by the medical students."

I grabbed his hand and lab coat then dug my finger nails into him and pulled him down closer so he would hear every word I was about to say," You're the one who cut off my panties and now I don't have any to wear home! You leave me alone!"

The doctor spun around facing the door and stomped to the door and yelled "who told this patient about her resuscitation? Nurse! Get in here now!" His scarlet cheeks were puffed out like a blow fish. I giggled inside. The nurse came running in and he trumpeted the words, "who told her I cut off her underwear?"

"Hey!" I barked back at him with all the force I could muster. "I was watching from above and I saw you cut off my panties."

He spun back around facing me, "How could you see what I did? You were dead!" His face was scarlet with rage, "You tell me who told you." He was determined to win this argument but he would fail.

I smiled with the memory of the beauty I had seen and said "I floated above the bed and watched you pushing on my chest and someone put a tube down my throat. I saw you cut off my panties. Then I left and came here to visit with Grace."

He stomped out of the building with all the students and nurse trailing after like a gaggle of geese.

Grace began to laugh. "That is the most rewarding thing I have ever witnessed in my life. I bet they leave you alone."

"I hope so because it hurts when they stick their fingers in me." I climbed over the bed rail and climbed into Grace's bed and we had a good time talking. She was so small and frail. Then I realized we were not talking. I knew what she was saying without moving her mouth. I did not move my mouth. 'How could we be talking', I wandered. I did not care. I was sixteen years old going on seventeen and very naive. It would take years to understand all that had happened.

The next day the doctor came to my bedside and listened to my chest and tummy. He placed a brown paper bag on my bed turned without a word and walked out of the room. I peered inside the bag and something red was inside. I reached in and pulled out the prettiest red pair of panties I had ever seen. They had a lace butterfly on the front. I showed them to Grace and she approved. I left them lying on my bed folded so everyone could see the butterfly when they came in. I was so proud of the beautiful butterfly. I was beginning to feel like a butterfly that had struggled out of my cocoon.

CHAPTER 7

I SAW THE BEAUTY
OF HIS SPIRIT.

A couple of days later the big black man came to visit me and had a large vase with beautiful flowers. I felt a love for this man I never knew I could muster. I could feel his kindness and empathy as a glowing halo of warmth emanating from him. It was a light that was in constant motion. At that moment I remembered learning that some people come into this life to be kind to others who are living through a life plan of selling their body for money. He was a kind pimp who protected the girls. The reasons for these girls and women life choices were many. They were simply living as planned. Some had been abused as children and knew no other way to find love. Others were here to teach tolerance and acceptance by their family who wanted to learn to change attitudes.

"I am glad to see you are doing so well, Miss Rita." He said shyly. Gentleness oozed from him like a beautiful rainbow fountain.

"Thank you for bringing me to the hospital. How did you know I was sick?" I quizzed.

"I heard you crying and moaning through the wall and I knew something was wrong. I have never heard noise through that wall before." He smiled exposing his beautiful ivories. I saw the beauty of his spirit. He left and said he would see me again. I closed my eyes and marveled at the aura of so many beautiful colors swirling about him. I thought I had seen the most beautiful flowers at my mom's cousin's florist shop. The colors around him were much more brilliant.

At that moment I realized when we are born into this earth plane, we do not remember what life had been like before. I knew somehow this is part of the perfect plan. Each time we return to earth we choose to advance all the way to the Bliss of Heaven and someday remain with the ALL and I AM. I hoped this was my time to reach that sublime level so I would not need to come back here.

A man in a suit came in and sat in the chair by my bed. He flipped open a notebook, took something from his pocket and took the top off the ink pen and said, "I understand you think you had an experience while you were being revived. I would like you to tell me what you think you saw".

I just stared at him and I saw a menacing, whirling fountain of gray and browns cascading from the top of his head and returning to his body from below. I felt my spirit actually recoiling away from him. The thought 'this girl is going to be committed' emanated from him. I had a friend who had to be admitted to a mental institution and I did not want to go there.

"What are you talking about?" I asked.

"Your doctor asked me to speak with you about what you experienced. Can you tell me what happened?" He leaned a little closer to my bed.

I put on my best puzzled look I could muster and replied "I wish I knew what you are talking about. What are you talking about?"

"I am a psychiatrist and I am here to help you understand what happened to you while you were being revived. You told your doctor that you saw what they were doing to you when you died?"

Well! That was point blank. At least he was being honest and I no longer saw any colors emanating from him.

My puzzled expression continued as I interjected, "I am trying to remember what you are talking about but I can't. What did he say again"? I was playing this guy pretty cool I thought. My intuition was strong.

The psychiatrist closed his notebook, put the top back on his pen and stood up and said, "If you remember what you saw tell the nurse and she will call me so we can talk about it." I resolved to never talk about this to anyone again. After-all, it would just land me in a mental institution.

It was many years later before I was able to recall more of what I learned while on the side of Heaven.

Another memory fluttered in to help me change the subject. It is funny how my mind can do that sometimes.

I was about 5 years old and mom wanted to go to my grandma's, and I wanted to go. She was driving the pickup truck and there was no room inside because she had things for grandma in it. I begged to ride in the back of the pickup. Mom let me and was very determined that I understood to remain sitting on the floor of the bed against the cab of the truck. I promised I would.

I could not see over the sides so I watched the clouds and how they changed shapes. Looking for shapes in the clouds was one of my favorite games. The wind whipped my hair around and I blinked often from the heavy breeze. Then everything went dark.

I opened my eyes to see a little slit of light. I was lying down on something soft. I could not move. My arms were pinned to my sides and I just lay there. Then the slit of light became bigger and then I could hear my mother calling my name in sobs and asking 'Jesus keep my baby alive'. Soon she lifted a board off me and reached in and picked me up. There was lumber lying everywhere. A small load of lumber was in the pickup beside me but I did not pay attention to it. Mom put some of the things from the cab to the back of the truck and me inside the cab and we went to grandma's house. We only had about a half mile to go.

Inside the house mom and grandma examined me all over. Mom told grandma, "I hit a big hole in the road and everything in the back flew out of the bed of the truck to the side of the road." She told her I landed first in a very grassy spot that had an oval grassy hole that just fit my body. The boards did not touch me. They simply held me still while my mother uncovered me and I was safe again. Grandma knelt down and began to pray thanks giving for keeping me totally safe. Grandma was a very spiritual lady and was one of the cornerstones of our Catholic Church in Idaho. I don't know what ever happened to the lumber.

CHAPTER 8

HEAVEN TALKS BACK

In the fall of 1967 I had such a compelling need to spend time with my mom. Joe, my husband said he could tell I was extremely restless and needed to do something. To my surprise he helped by getting me set up for my trip on the train to go to Idaho from a city in Kansas. He was working as a law enforcement officer for Santa Fe Rail Road (Railroad Bull) at the time. Joe put in for his vacation for the last two weeks of the month and I would then drive home with him. My mother had gotten a divorce from my dad a year or two earlier and she had married a man named Bud. I got off the train at the tiny Union Pacific Rail Road station in the middle of nowhere in our county in Idaho. I was the only person who got off the train. I looked both ways across the gravel road and saw a car and a man was standing in front of it. I began walking toward him and he turned to me and smiled. The hairs on the back of my neck stood up more than they ever had. I was walking toward some sort of evil presence. I was not sure if I wanted to get in the car with this man. I could not understand what was happening. I just knew I would not become friends with him.

He said, "Hi! I'm Bud! Are you Rita?" My heart sunk. I wished this was not the man my mom married. But deep inside a little voice said, 'she is living her life plan.' I sighed and walked over, and let him take my bag and open the passenger door for me. He drove the to the North Side, which is an area north of our town where farm land had been opened up when I was little. Two of my uncles had big farms out there and my mother had a combination store, cafe and laundromat that served most of the farmers and hired hands in the area. It was a long drive into town. Most of the hired hands were itinerant works from Mexico and Native American Navajo Indians from the four corners area of New Mexico, Arizona, Nevada and Utah.

I walked in and there was mom standing behind the counter. She came around and we were in a long embrace for what seemed like five minutes. It seemed it had been a long time since

I had seen her. I was going to spend a whole month with my mom and brothers and sisters. I enjoyed many good times with my siblings. It was sad they were too young to remember much of when I lived at home. It turned out later that so many of them had distorted memories that were planted day by day by my father.

One day in the cafe when no-one was around, Mom and I just visited with each other cantered happily with each other joking and have a good old-fashion blast together. Somehow the subject of dying came up.

Mom said to me, "If something happens to me that will leave me unable to do anything or care for myself or my family I want you to promise to let me go."

Huh? Where did that come from? I was startled. "Why would you say something like that Mom?" I asked. I threw a wet dish cloth at her.

She grabbed the cloth, "I just felt like I needed to ask you to do this for Me." she said in her playful tone. I was suspicious because my mom was very intuitive.

I retorted back with, "OK! Then you have to promise to talk and communicate with me when you are in heaven". I caught a rag she threw at me and made ready to throw it back.

"Hum! OK! I will!" she promised, "And if things happen in threes, remember it is me communicating with you." She caught the rag I threw to her.

As time passed it was apparent that life was not all good for my mother in her marriage. No matter how hard I tried to get mom to talk to me about what was going on she would not tell me. When Bud walked in I could feel the tension emitting from mom. I was helpless to do anything. Again, the thought deep within said 'she is living her life plan.' One evening I looked out the back door and mom and Bob where in her car. Her blouse was torn and she was crying.

"Mom," I yelled, "I need your help right now!" She got out of the car and I stepped back into a full restaurant and said "Bud is beating up my mother." Nearly every male in the cafe jumped up and ran to their vehicles and chased after Bud. I was satisfied. My mother was devastated. I felt a pang of joy as I saw the number of people who thought that much of my mother that they would go after the man who was bullying her.

I still had not told anyone of my near death experience. I did not want people to think I was crazy.

My husband Joe came and spent the last two weeks of my stay with the family and then we drove back to Kansas. When I arrived at home it was in the afternoon, November 1, 1967. It had been a sixteen hour drive and I was tired. I thought I would let the unpacking and laundry wait until tomorrow. There was something nagging at me and I was compelled to get the laundry done. So I did.

The next day I was putting the last of the laundry away and the telephone rang. It was from the hospital in our small town in Idaho.

November 2, 1967, A nurse said "Your mother is in the hospital and you were the only relative in the United States who we could locate who is over twenty-one years old. So I called you". My brother was in the Army in Germany. All the rest of my siblings were under twenty-one. She said "I am putting the phone up to the doctor's ear."

A male voice was on the other side and he introduced himself as the emergency room doctor. He said that my mother had been in an automobile accident and was not doing well. In fact she was losing more blood than they could pump into her. "Your mother gave us your phone number so that you may instruct me to stop the life saving efforts. She said you would understand" My heart sank and I felt numb.

Was this a joke? Then the doctor said "your mother's leg and hip have been nearly severed off. We cannot repair the damage."

I could hear mom in the background, "Please Rita, tell them to stop. Remember your promise". I was in suspended animation. I could feel nothing but I could picture my mother throwing that rag at me and I promised her. The entire month together with her played back in my mind in an instant.

I said, "Stop. Do not do any more to keep her alive." I remained in that suspension as if I was nowhere. My mind was very acute as all other thoughts and feelings were blocked from my awareness.

I heard my mother call out, "Thank you, Rita, I love you, I'm ready Jesus. Oh yes I am ready Jesus, Jesus is here for me Rita."

The doctor asked if I was still on the line and I said I was. "She is gone. She is resting with Jesus now." He said in a somber voice. "I am truly sorry for the loss of your mother. She has been a pillar of our community."

I hung up the phone and called the train station and was transferred to Joe's office. I told him what happened and he came straight home. I was already putting the clothes back into the travel bags. We drove back for the funeral. Joe called the only dealership in my little home town in Idaho that a car would be towed to and asked them to put mom's car behind locked doors until he got there. When we got to Idaho the car had been dismantled and scattered around the salvage yard over 500 square yardage area. If any malicious damage had been done to the car, it was lost. There would be no way to prove our suspicions that Bud had done something to the brakes on Mom's car. The funeral was one of the largest in the history of our town.

We tried to keep the restaurant open while living in the apartment in back. After a couple of weeks we were visited by the local Sheriff's office with an eviction notice. We were to be out by midnight. The deputy took the cash register with him. All we could do was pack. Bud was kicking us out. I called one of my uncles explaining the situation and he said he could do nothing. I wanted to take my brothers and sisters back with me to Kansas to live but my mother's brothers and sisters said no. I was willing to stay and keep the farm going and the family together. We were poor so we had no money to hire an attorney.

In December of 1969 two of my brothers came to live with us.

Four years after Mom's death, April 10 1971, I was washing dishes when all of a sudden I heard my mother's voice saying, "Rita".

I answered in that sarcastic way that a miss-behaved teenager would respond with "What!" I froze and stared straight ahead then turned my head to the living room. My mind flew through all scenarios including 'am I hearing things?' But that voice was loud and real. I had heard my mother. It was difficult to reconcile my mind. I don't know how long I stood there but the dish water grew cold when I came back to moment.

I continued to wash the dishes when I heard her again. "Rita, Margaret is alright." Her voice was clear and there was no mistake.

"Mom?" I said in an almost inaudible voice. "What do you mean?" Somehow I found myself sitting in the living room. I do not remember walking into the living room.

Another five minutes past and I heard her again. "Margaret is alright!" my mother's voice was clear and strong. I sat there mesmerized for an unknown amount of time. My sister Margaret was living in Oregon and I was living in a little town in New Mexico. My daughter was eighteen months old. She was sleeping in the playpen in the living room.

My spell was broken when the telephone rang. Aunt Clara was on the phone. "Rita. Margaret is dying and you need to fly to Portland, Oregon right away." she said in a quivering voice. I was unable to say anything for a moment and she said, "Rita. Did you hear me? Margaret was in an accident and she is in the hospital." Clara is my mother's sister and she lived in Idaho. It was clear that she was upset.

I took a deep breath, smiled and said "Margaret is alright. She is going to be okay", I answered in a matter of fact voice.

"Rita, I told you. You need to make arrangements to fly out before she dies." She was crying and disparately trying to make me understand.

"Aunt Clara, please calm down. Margaret is alright. Mom just talked to me and said so."

"Rita, what is the matter with you! Your mother is dead. She could not talk to you." she was almost yelling over the phone. Then she asked, "Is Joe there?"

"No he is out working." My husband was the Town Marshall of Hancock, New Mexico.

I heard a loud sigh and Aunt Clara said, "Write this down. You tell Joe to call me when he gets in. Here is my phone number." She hung up the phone and I sat there with a smile. I understood why my mom came to me. She is keeping her promise to communicate with me.

Later Joe came in for refreshment and I told him what happened with my mother and the call from Aunt Clara. I gave him the phone number. He asked me to dial it as he put a slice of ham on his sandwich. I could hear the phone ringing at the other end. Aunt Clara answered "Hi Aunt Clara. Joe is here so you can talk to him now." I heard a gasp on the other end of the line.

I handed the phone to Joe and he said, "OK. That sounds good. Sure, I'll tell her." and he hung up the phone. "Well" he said. "Margaret is going to be OK. I guess the first phone call to relatives was premature. She was riding on the back of a motorcycle and the guy she was with died at the scene. His body buffered the impact for Margaret. She does have a compound fracture of her leg." he smiled at me and said, "Your mother was just in time. She sure saved us money." We were living day to day, paycheck to paycheck at the time.

We both were relieved and I gave thanks for my sister being alive and OK. Often I will look up and just say "Thank You". In fact, I try to do it every morning. I thank God for no reason: Just a Thank you for everything.

I graduated from nursing school in May of 1977. God was not done using me. My life plan had much more in the tapestry to complete.

I was working in the intensive care (ICU) at a Hospital in New Mexico in the late 1990's when a young man was brought into the hospital. He had a self inflicted gunshot wound to his head. All the tests showed that he was brain dead. We had him on full life support. My husband and his father were personal friends. The parents were in and out of the hospital room. After a couple of hours passed I asked them both to sit with me. I had let them grieve and lament and now I wanted to discuss organ donations. At first they were reluctant, especially the mother. I continued to sit with them.

After a ten minute wait of not speaking I asked, "What do you think your son would want right now if he was whispering in your ear? What if one person could have a new lease on life because of a new kidney, or a little girl could play again because of your son's heart?" I paused again and said nothing.

I could see the mother relaxing and she turned to her husband and said "I think he wants us to donate his organs". Then he asked, "Do you have anything we need to sign? Their faces seemed more relaxed as if a part of the grieving process had passed. Could they have reached the level of acceptance so soon?

They signed the papers and I called the supervisor to come to the ICU. She took the papers away and soon returned saying that the local two prop plane they usually hired was getting ready to transport the donor to The University of New Mexico Hospital.

Sister the supervisor used the phone in the ICU as called many numbers trying to find a nurse to go on the flight with the donor. Ours was a small town and available nurses were limited. My shift was just finishing and I stood beside her. I felt compelled to offer since this was the son of friends. "Sister, I will go."

Sister swirled around as her habit ballooned out as she jumped into high gear. She called a nurse's aide (as we called them in those days) who had been on many air flights with patients, to ride with me since I had never flown with a patient. She wanted her along to help me get through it without a problem. I went with the young man on the ambulance as I kept control of his critical intravenous (IV) lines and I bagged him with the ambu bag through his intubation tube keeping him breathing. It was critical to keep all organs open and blood and fluids flowing. I could not allow any cavity or tubule to malfunction in the organs. The nurse's aide arrived at the airport and I climbed on first. The pilot had removed two seats on the left side of the plane and the ambulance crew and the pilot anchored the gurney onto the brackets where the seats had been. I took over the ambu bag and continued the breathing process for him. It was important to keep the intravenous lines (I Vs) under control so I checked them often. I was unable to buckle in because of the way I had to sit to keep the IVs and Urine flow visible and breathing for him. The nurse aid settled back and closed her eyes in the seat behind me. She had just gotten off duty on the prior shift so had only been off about eight hours when she got the call.

I was so busy with my duties keeping everything going that I barely noticed we were off the ground. The engine was so loud I could hear nothing. I kept my concentration on what I was doing and I could feel the plane moving around in the air reminding me when I would ride on my uncles speed boat on the Snake River in Idaho when I was little, with the bounces and jerking around. At one point something hit me in the head and it hurt but I kept up what I was doing.

A loud hissing sound broke my concentration and the nurse aid said. "Get this thing on the ground now. We have a broken oxygen bottle."

The small oxygen tubing that was in the face mask of the ambu was gone but I continued, counting out loud more for my concentration "One, two, three, four! One, two, three, four!" I knew he was still getting oxygen from the room air. I had changed out IV bags several times on the flight, the urine flow was adequate, and the donor's chest would rise with each squeeze of the bag. I felt a bump and I could tell we were on the ground. An ambulance came roaring over to our plane along with a fire truck. The side door opened and a man began unfastening the gurney from the brackets and a fireman stood ready. They took over the IV s and put the patient on a respirator and I jumped into the ambulance to go with him. I had all the paper work and I wanted to be able to report back to his family that he made it in good condition.

The nurse aid was in the ambulance and she kept muttering. "We flipped over and over. Can you believe it, we flipped over and over." Her eyes were wide and she was in distress. I did not comprehend what she was saying. My attention was on my patient.

We arrived at the hospital and I was directed to the doctor's lounge and the hospital staff took over. The ambulance promised to wait for me and get me back to the plane for a ride home. I gave a report to an intern and gave them report on the events leading to our arrival. I left the information of the donor's family requesting that they at least contact them with any results, such as; a fifteen year old received his heart from their kind gift, etc. I was assured that they would notify the family about every part they were able to transplant. A nurse took time to write down the family information, address and phone number.

I went out to our ambulance and I said I was ready to go back to the airport. I could not see the nurse aid that had come with me. The driver said she left and took a bus home. I said my good-byes and thanks to the ambulance crew and boarded the little plane to go back home. I wanted to sit back and enjoy the ride. The pilot said he was sure happy to see me. I asked why. "Your companion, left here saying she would never ride with me again. It looks like she meant it."

I know."I answered. "They told me she took a bus home."

The pilot chuckled. "Do you want to sit in front with me? I have something to tell you. Also I will give a wonderful ride home."

I climbed into the seat beside him with the anticipation of a child getting ready for a wonderful carnival ride and soon we were in the air. It was after three in the morning and the moon was almost full. He took us above the clouds and I was fascinated. Then he came down a little and we flew over several small towns and villages. I was able to name most of them. "OK." The pilot said, "Now I think I need to tell you what happened. The wind came up over the mountains at Albuquerque and spun us around and I tried hard to pull up and over the turbulence and the plane rolled three times. The oxygen tank was leaking and I radioed for a mayday and a fast decent into Albuquerque. We made the fasted landing in the history of the Albuquerque airport." he paused and then took a breath and said, "What happened to us was a miracle. We should have crashed into the Sandia Mountains. I don't know why we didn't but I am grateful. I just thought you should know."

I looked at him and said, "It was a good thing I am the one who took this assignment. It is not my time to go. I have angels watching over me. I suppose I should tell you, this is the very first time I have ever been up in a plane."

We arrived back in home and he drove me to the hospital to get my car. The trip played over and over in my mind. I would never forget this. I giggled with joy because of flying. I wondered what Sister Mary would have said if she had known I had never flown before.

Around the year nineteen and eight five (1985), I was working at the at another hospital, New Mexico. I had a knack for starting intravenous lines. The hospital was so small we did not have a pediatric unit so most children that came were on the regular medical floor. I was asked to start an IV on a little boy who had been admitted to medical floor. I walked into his room. Something seemed familiar about him. His mother was sitting on a chair on the other side of the bed. I sat on his bed and began to prepare him for the injection when he said, "Wow! It is you! You are prettier than when you were red."

His mother said, "Oh! Don't pay him any mind. He does that all the time with some people." I felt a little rub of uneasiness toward his mother as I wanted to disagree with her. Why did I feel that way?

A sliver of a memory came to me of a red planet with red skinned people, and two moons in the sky. "Oh yes! How have you been?" I asked. I felt a kinship and realization that I had been on that planet with this boy's spirit. I cannot explain it anymore but I still remember that moment and the utter happiness of seeing him again. "It's OK, your mom just doesn't understand" I said.

CHAPTER 9

PROOF I HAVE ANGELS

Angels have no Religion or Phylosophy.
Angels are our helpers, guides and healers if
we let them. We must ask for their help. They
are always ready to help.. Rita D Lovins

Years passed. My grandfather died. I called my
grandmother and to my surprise she was giddy
and joyful. She said that 'Pop had gotten up in
the middle of the night and was talking.' This is
her story: "I told Pop to go back to bed because
he was talking in the middle of the night. He
told me he was talking to Edna, your mother.
I told him Edna is dead and to go back to bed.
He said he knew Edna was dead but she was
here to take him with her. He kept talking to no
one and I told him again to go to bed. Then he
said, "OK! Edna. I better go back to bed before

Mom has a conniption fit. I will be with you in a minute". I thought nothing of it but when I went to get him up this morning he was dead. So he is in heaven. Isn't it wonderful? I agreed with her and I told her I knew he was in heaven with my mom. We cried together and talked about the wonderful times we had with my grandfather and my mother.

I had my beautiful daughter was born in May, 1970. The joys of motherhood enveloped my life. In the seventies I was blessed with my two brothers who came to live with us. Each came when they were in the ninth grade. My stepson lived with us on and off throughout the years and he was with us until my daughter was two years old.

It was during this time that the boys began selling Grit Magazine. I was reading one of the issues and an article reported about a man in Canada who had died and his family was kneeling around his bed praying for him. The doctor had come to the house and pronounced him dead. He woke up nearly a half hour later and described what he saw that was so close to my encounter that I told my husband about my near death experience. For the first time I realized I was not crazy and it was real. It had been so many years (so I thought) that I could not remember many of the details.

At age thirty two I graduated from nursing school and spent many years in my career. I read the stories that Dr. Elizabeth *Kubler-Ross* had written about the stages of dying and more of her works. This promoted me to learn all I could about my experience. I found the book 'Life After Life' by Raymond Moody. Most of what he found from interviewing one-hundred and fifty people was as follows:

(a) an overwhelming feeling of peace and well-being, including freedom from pain.
(b) the impression of being located outside one's physical body.
(c) floating or drifting through darkness, sometimes described as a tunnel.
(d) becoming aware of a golden light.
(e) encountering and perhaps communicating with a "being of light".
(f) having a rapid succession of visual images of one's past.
(g) experiencing another world of much beauty.

Wikipedia. And www.lifeafterlife.com

I continued to study which took me into the world of physics, quantum physics, Eastern, Christian and metaphysical studies. I talked about writing a book for many years but when I set it down on paper I hit block after block. I was not ready. I had not lived long enough for my physical brain to comprehend what had happened while I was on the other side of the veil (in Heaven).

In the year 2000 I was working at a minimum security prison in New Mexico when I began falling. Inmates would rush to my side and pick me up and carry me back to the medical clinic. I had a boss who was in another facility about two hundred miles away. He found out what was happening. Arthur called me and asked what was happening. I explained I was falling and the doctors in Town could not figure out why. He told me to take the week off and he would get back with me about what to do next.

The following day Arthur, my boss called and had made an appointment with the company doctor in Albuquerque. I had many tests done that were not pleasant and in the end I was diagnosed with Post Polio Syndrome. My muscles were weakening and soon I was using a walker and then an electric scooter to get around. The pain of walking more than two hundred feet became unbearable. And with that I would have to stop and rest for a minute before continuing about four times during that walk.

September, 11 2001, I was driving to my doctor's office because I was having strange pains in my neck and shortness of breath. They were the classic signs of an impending myocardial infarction (Heart Attack) in women. When I arrived at the office everyone was gathered around the television. 'What was going on'! I inquired.

The World Trade Center had been hit by planes. "See? Watch they are showing it again," a voice came from the crowd.

"What country is it in?" I asked.

"It is in New York City." Several chimed in unison.

I was speechless as I watched and then a tower collapsed and soon the other. I will never forget where I was when the towers came down.

I had been having difficulty for a couple of weeks with the front of my neck throat area. A week prior to my doctor visit my girlfriend from across the street was visiting and I began to feel faint. My esophagus felt strange and I stroked it. My breathing became labored. I asked my friend to get an allergy pill and an aspirin out of my medicine cabinet and give them to me fast. I had been an intensive care nurse for several years and I knew the signs of both coronary events and severe allergies. I was not going to take any chances. I remember waking up sitting in my recliner and firemen in their yellow suits and hats were walking around my house. I had oxygen on my face and a blood pressure cuff was on my arm. A heart monitor was attached to my chest. They put me on a gurney and soon I was on my way to the hospital. At the hospital I was interviewed by an intern. I wondered why I had not had a NDE at that time.

It had been raining heavily that day and several women had come into the emergency department with severe allergies. They were treated and sent home. The doctor of the day came in to say hello as we knew each other. He came to Roswell when I was a nurse in this very hospital. He said my symptoms pointed to the allergies and since I was doing well now it must be that the allergy pill had done the trick. He signed off on my chart and sent me home. I had offered my arm several times for blood tests. None were ever taken.

A week later, I had a scan and a couple weeks later I was in a Hospital in Albuquerque having angioplasty with a stint inserted in my right coronary artery. The doctor who inserted the catheter was watching the screen and said, "This artery is ninety-nine percent occluded. She should be dead. What is keeping this woman alive?" he had forgotten that I was not sedated and only under a mild sedative.

"I have angels, Doctor. They will not let me die." I said matter-of-fact, and the room was suddenly silent. The doctor apologized for what he said.

Amused, I answered him, "That's OK doctor. I have been in the operating room too and we have to talk and tell jokes. Do you have any good jokes?" the people around me chuckled and seemed to relax into a jovial mood.

One of the nurses said, "Her chart mentions she is a registered nurse."

I went back home to and kept my appointment with the Cardiac specialist. That clinic was open four days a week. The doctor that worked in our little town two days a week had just given a seminar to the doctors in the area, a month prior to my admission, to the emergency department. He was livid and said he will be taking each doctor aside and explaining how close they came to a big law suit. That was another time I was to remain on the earth for now. It was not my time to go. We all have our own time we are to go.

CHAPTER 10

FORTH TRIP TO HEAVEN

I learned we all know how to live a wonderfully Divine life because we all have done it before. We all came here from the heavenly rhelm to bring a Divine life to this planet. When we were born we forgot where we came from or at least the memory began to fade. Some who have come begin to remember why we came into this lifetime and our focus in life changes dramatically. We are here to make changes in our own life and the life of others. We are all Divine Energy and with that energy we radiate our inner knowing and being. We all effect the world around us. If we only understood the power of your thought you would be ever so careful what you think. Start with Love and all the rest will fall into place as you progress in this life and the next. Have you walked into a room and felt the joy and gaity of the people around you? Or have you walked into a place and felt the negative uncomfortable stress that is so thick you want to leave? I begin each morning by saying Thank you and then I do my little centering and short meditation which brings in Love and then eminates love from me to all that is around me. This love emination usually extends about 5 to 10 feet around you. Some very advanced souls are able to extend that field to encompass the entire universe. I hope to reach that level of Love Energy.

My daughter purchased a home on a mountain east of Albuquerque so that we could move in with her and be close to specialists. I was no longer able to do all the activities of daily living such as cooking and cleaning. I was told by the experts to stop and pace myself or I would lose what I have left of my mobility. The house had a wing off to the side and she thought we could live there.

That winter we had a record snow fall. My lungs began to tighten up in the middle of the night. I got up and moved to the living room where I could sit up to rest and make my breathing a little easier. I slipped out of my body once more and I was so trilled. Yes! I was ready to go. Life was no longer very pleasant for me.

I wanted it to end and just stay on the beautiful side of the veil.

I saw my body sitting with my upper body propped on pillows on the couch as I floated away and toward the light. The speed I traveled was faster than before. It was almost instantaneous. I was greeted by all my wonderful friends and helpers. Again I believe I saw Jesus, Mary his mother, Mary Magdalene, Melchizedek, Dom Ignacio' who is known as St Ignatius Loyola, Abraham, St Francis of Assisi, Lao Tze, and a few other teachers who had come to the earth plane in the past. Yet! They were shaking their heads 'no'. "What? Not again! I don't want to go back to earth!" I felt myself say. Then a beautiful being embraced me and said I had to return to finish my task. I needed to help people and tell them of the beauty of heaven and the whole story.

'But I cannot remember the whole story!' I lamented.

Love enveloped me and said the 'memories will now begin to come'. I will be guided to the right teachers and studies to help me with my teachings. I must pay attention to my inner voice and promptings.

Suddenly I was back in my body and my daughter was shaking me yelling, "Mom! Mom! Are you all right?"

I was having difficulty breathing. She called the emergency medical system, EMS. It took quite awhile for the ambulance to get to me. The winter was one of the areas record snow falls. A snow plow was pressed into service with the ambulance following to get to my daughter's house on top of the mountain. In the hospital it was determined I had pneumonia. My oxygen levels were so low that they said they were surprised I was living. My oxygen level was 35 and it must be 90 or higher. I continued on oxygen for over a year. I was unable to continue living on the mountain because of the altitude, so my husband and I moved into an assisted living faculty in another town in New Mexico.

I began writing bits and pieces of my near death experiences in tablets. I wrote page after page but was unable to put them together in a meaningful way. I then graduated to a power chair while living in our second assisted living facility. I fell into a spiral of negative energy and I realized I was not happy and was quite negative in my speech and actions. I was not a fun person to be around. Sitting in the dining room with our usual dinner partners, I made a negative comment about the food. The man said that they would be sitting with someone else from now on. "You are too critical of everything. You are not fun to be around anymore." He told me in a stern voice that hit me like ice water splashing in my face. At first I was angry and then I began to reflect on this and I realized he was right. My own daughter had told me the same thing. It all began many years before when I began having repulsive feelings toward my husband. I will not go into the reasons in this book. This is not the time to discuss that branch of my life if ever. I was angry because I was becoming weaker with my post-polio syndrome. I had gained weight and of course it made it even more difficult to walk. I did not like my life. I sunk into depression.

We eventually moved back to Albuquerque for the specialists available into an apartment when I was doing a little better because we needed to live where our money would stretch so we could live at least with good food. Assisted Living Facilities are very expensive. In 2003, my doctor told me I would probably be in a nursing facility for total care by the year 2005. I became more depressed. A strange thing happened! I began to have memories of my Near-Death-Experience. I had a vision that I was walking and enjoying life.

After spending about a month sinking deeper into depression a thought came to me from no where.

"What have I got to loose?" My doctor would not order rehabilitation for me. I had completed my occupational therapy which helped me learn to function with the limited use of my legs and arms. I could ride the bus nearly anywhere in Albuquerque. I decided to try to do my own rehabilitation. I obtained a large stretch band and began working my legs and arms. Our apartment building had a heated swimming pool. The only problem I had was navigating down five steps to the level of the pool and edging myself along the wall with a ledge to the pool hand rail. I would lower myself into the pool and slowly and over time exercise in the warm water. The hardest part was getting out of that pool. With each step out of the buoyancy the heavier my legs became. In the beginning it took me forty five minutes to get back to my power-chair. The pain in my legs and arms had me in tears. I persisted with the thought that I would end up in a nursing home or I would get out of that chair and walk.

In the fall of 2004, I had started on Saturday night calls with Mike after the special free mentoring calls. Mike facilitated a support group of people learning to overcome obstacles in life. I learned I had a very low self-esteem which began in my childhood and continued throughout my life.

I learned a wonderful lesson from my mentor, Mike to stand in front of a mirror and say out loud every morning and night, 'I Love You!' At first the practice was difficult but I persisted.

At first I did not feel the words to be true but I continued every day. As time passed I began to notice wrinkles softening on my face. I saw less melancholy eyes staring back at me. Today I have total love for myself and for all. I am not usually bothered by insults as I know that the person is just on his or her path. I do send Love to all and bless them. This too is another story for the future. A group I joined with Mike, was going on a cruise in the fall of 2005 and I wanted to go with them. I saved my money from January 2005. I also was able to get room for a friend I had come to know on the internet who was legally blind. Mike told me I had to get out of that chair so I could enjoy the cruise with all the fun things they had planned.

July of 2005 I got out of that power chair for the last time. That too will be another book in the future. I was so sure I would walk again that I took continuing education and the tests to get my nursing license back up to date. I had my nursing license back up and ready for another two years. In June.

In September, I started working for a nursing agency and worked part time and later I worked at a couple of hospitals in New Mexico. My husband, Joe, died in the later part of November. I continued to work as a nurse with renewed vigor.

I began writing this book on my laptop computer. In September of 2006 I met George whom I married in June of 2007. I had to start this book from scratch several times because of computer crashes and computer glitches.

Each time I started over, more memories came flooding back. It was as if each computer crash was part of the plan in order to exercise my brain and spirit to come through with the occurrences in my near death experiences (NDE).

In January 2009 I again had to stop working and got back on disability. It was a sad time for me but new adventures began to take shape. We somehow became more like a gypsy couple traveling every one or two years to a new destination. I had a need to see many places. Circumstances in life took us to many places to help others. There were people I was supposed to meet and tell my story.

We spent the latter half of September 2010 through 2011 with my daughter and her family. Erika was at her wits end as she had three small children, one had multiple food allergies and would end up in the hospital with life threatening anaphylactic shock and the baby who had been born premature with Down Syndrome in April 2010 would go to the hospital near death with respiratory problems. Those hospital stays would last from four days to two weeks. We spent many weeks with the children who remained at home during those hospital stays. It was such a pleasure to be with my family and help out with the children. Finally the children were improving. The old saying that two women cannot live in the same kitchen is true. It was so hard to leave but I was forced to follow my path. When the spirit pushes I have to move. Never be angry about any condition that forces you to make changes.

I finally purchased a San-disc flash drive to keep my book and now I can complete what I started. I became more attune to the idea that losing the book those many times was a good thing.

CHAPTER 11

MOVE TO MEXICO

In December of 2013 we traveled to Puerto Vallarta Mexico for a vacation. We both fell in love with Mexico. I felt like I was home and we began looking for apartments. I was looking on the internet and found an apartment in the Lake Chapala, Mexico area. There was something about the pictures that drew me in. I knew I wanted to live there for awhile. I contacted the owner and we made an appointment to meet her. We rented a car and packed almost everything we had and drove to Lake Chapala the next morning. We arrived late in the evening and the owners land lady came when we called to let us see the apartment. I had a strong intuition we would remain in the Lake Chapala area. I expressed my feeling to her and she seemed to understand. I told her about my book and I wanted a quiet place to write. As it worked out we were able to put a deposit on it and we were able to stay in the apartment even though it was not quite finished with the remodeling. She told me I would be inspired as the lake is considered a strong vortex.

In two days we stowed most of our belongings in the apartment. The trip back to Puerto Vallarta was rot with obstacles. Somehow we missed the toll road and the trip was much longer than anticipated but the mountains were astonishingly beautiful. We finally came to a junction and got on the toll road. Everything was running smoothly when all of a sudden climbing a mountain the car slowed and made a puffing sound and stopped. We had heard many horror stories about Mexico so we were both a bit on edge and then I said "We are going to be OK."

Within fifteen minutes a three quarter ton truck pulled up and a man got out, walked over to the car and motioned for us to open the hood of the car. He wiggled some wires then brought out jumper cables. All attempts failed to get that little car started. I pulled out my car rental papers to find a phone number. My cell phone would not work in those mountains. The man got back in his truck and sat there. Soon a very large pickup pulled up with 2 men on the back with menacing looking guns. My mind raced with thoughts such as, are we going to die? Are we going to be robbed. We had been warned by people in the states to be careful in Mexico because they like to kill foreigners. I am sure I was pale with fear and I don't remember much else until: In about ten minutes a truck came with a flat bed. The driver backed up to the little car and lowered the bed. He got out and both men placed chains to the frame and pulled the car up onto the bed. We were helped into the tow truck. I was feeling more and more relaxed. Silently, I looked up and 'Thank You'.

We stopped at a toll station and a paramedic came to greet me. He dialed the car rental place from his land line in his office and they were given our location. He hung up and said it will be about three hours. I was welcome to sit with him in the office.

I learned so much from him about Mexico. He told me that since I had paid to be on the toll road I was under Federal protection of Mexico and they would take care of me. Even if we needed to be hospitalized we would be covered just because we had our toll ticket. He said that ticket is insurance. The Federal government of Mexico goes to great lengths to protect us especially on the toll road.

We saw large and small trucks drive by with armed soldiers on the back. Those guns were not the run of the mill guns. They were machine guns.

An interesting tidbit he gave me was that the government had designated about three or four areas where the cartels may carry on their business as long as they do not harass or molest the innocent especially the foreigners. He had lots of questions for me when I told him I am a nurse. The three hours turned into four but they passed quickly. Finally a car came with two young men. They tried to use jumper cables on the car to no avail. We all climbed into their small car and they drove four hours back to the apartment near Puerto Vallarta.

The next day we flew back to New Mexico to get the rest of our belongings. We planned to drive our car to Lake Chapala. Of course we drove around and visited with some family members in the USA for about two weeks. We spent two days in El Paso Texas, at the Mexican Immigration and got our papers for permanent residence in Mexico.

CHAPTER 12

WHY CREATION? MY LESSONS BEGIN

"In each atom, in each corpuscle, is life. Life is what you worship as God ... and earth is only an atom in the universe of worlds." - Edgar Cayce

I want to thank Edgar Cayce A.R.E for your help. *http://www.edgarcayce.org/*

Memories of the lessons I learned are manifesting as if on Cue as I write this account. My big question was 'how and why were we created in the first place. I had heard many reasons as I grew up. I was told by the nuns at our Catholic training that we were created to Adore God.

I am smiling because I know that the great lesson that Jesus wanted us to learn is that we too shall rise after death. Death is just a step to the other side.

I learned we were created to adore God. I also learned that we should all listen to our clergy as they have all the answers for our salvation. I learned to fear God as a punishing God.

The reason for creation was far from anything I had learned or imagined. In-fact the reason was curiosity. The Infinite Being, sometimes called God, Divine Source, Allah, the Great Father, Adonai, YHWH, The Self-Existent One, Holy Ghost, Immanuel, Jahovah, JAH, King, OMEGA, YAH and called many names in many customs, had a spark of curiosity. We also learned God created us in his own image. That is truer than most believe. You see, we are all parts of that Source, God, and Infinite Being. The curiosity stemmed from the desire to see what would happen and what it would be like to spring forth as energy and matter. I must add a point here. When the springing forth (The Big Bang) came about, perfect balance and calculation were part of the pour energy into the physical. We as humans are learning that mathematical reasoning and more was in the creation. Teachers have talked to us about God being Love. It is true. God is more than that and it may take many lifetimes to understand such an idea.

Oh! Did you flinch when I said lifetimes? I have been told I am wrong to add this to my book. Reincarnation is a very important part of this book. But I do have to realize you made it this far into this book because of my statements about my other lives before this one.

I have a small example that shows no one ever said there is no such thing as reincarnation.

For westerners the following is for Christians taken from the Bible. Other faiths and customs already know the answer.

The Transfiguration

Mark 9-1. After six days Jesus took with him Peter, James and John the brother of James, and led them up a high mountain by themselves.

2: There he was transfigured before them. His face shone like the sun, and his became as white as the light. (We all have this white light waiting to manifest as Love)

3: Just then there appeared before them Moses and Elijah, talking with Jesus.

10: The disciples asked him, "Why then do the teachers of the law say that Elijah must come first?"

11: Jesus replied, "To be sure, Elijah comes and will restore all things.

1: 2 But I tell you, Elijah has already come, and they did not recognize him, but have done to him everything they wished. In the same way the Son of Man is going to suffer at their hands."

WOW! There it is. There is more in the Bible and other ancient books about reincarnation but I believe I will leave that to the reader to discover. There is much that is not in the Bible. Studying the translations from the ancient texts will bring more knowledge to the person who wishes to step out of his/her comfort zone and learn. Again we must remember that those who wrote down the word of mouth stories at a later time of Jesus either neglected some of what happened or the translations that followed lost much of the truth. I am not going to dwell on the point Jesus made about Elijah already coming and treated the same way Jesus was treated. I did not have the privilege to learn more about it.

I do know many of the bible scribes found knowledge in ancient texts from the orient. I leave it up to you to turn away and not believe or go forward and study.

We are living in a group and crossing paths with people we have enjoyed our lives with before both on this side and on the other side of the veil of heaven. When we are on the other side of the veil we rejoin our life tribe some who never reside on earth. We are greeted with wonderful ceremony and celebration when we get there. Someone very close to us is always there as we cross over and heading toward the light. The crossing is always wonderful and filled with pure Love.

Many times we cross the path of someone from our heavenly tribe for a moment and sometimes we pass by someone from a life in another dimension or planet. When God had the twinkle of curiosity, it did not focus just on this little M planet circling this sun we look at every day. We cannot see all the stars that contain life of any-kind from here. Our Hubble telescope cannot see that far. Our mind cannot begin to fathom the number of planets with life in existence now, in the past and to be developed in the future. Not all life forms are carbon based.

It is now time to make my bold statement again. We are all part of God and therefore God is part of us. What God can do we can do. When God had the "Curiosity Moment" and the word came forth to create all things the energy that came forth was God which burst forward from the first instant, and continues to expand. All of the God particles began to come together to form larger objects and we can look around us and see from our tiny point something of that happening thanks to modern technology.

John 10:34

New American Standard Bible
Jesus answered them, "Has it not been written in your Law, 'I SAID, YOU ARE GODS '?
King James Bible
Jesus answered them, Is it not written in your law, I said, Ye are gods?

I found another wonderful source of this information by Owen K Water in his "Discover Your Sacred Purpose in Life Course". When I read his account I was filled with an overwhelming feeling of validation. Someone else had learned the same as I had. I had not read it in other stories of Near Death Experiences. Before creation there was stillness and sublime bliss. There was total perfection. There really was no reason for creating except for that little nature called curiosity. If you think about it, curiosity is what keeps you learning and striving forth all these years.

Why are we here? What are we supposed to do? You need to understand that before Creation of the universe, and before the Divine Source became an active Creator, there was total bliss and stillness.

The last question is the real gem. It was the longest-standing mystery in the history of spiritual philosophy and you are about to realize the answer!

Before the Creation of the universe, before God became an active Creator, there was stillness and perfection. The original form of God was, and still is, infinite beingness {ET al}. This all-pervasive awareness is the deepest quality of consciousness within all beings. People call this original consciousness of all life the Godhead, the Absolute, the All That Is, Brahman, Tao, and many alternative names. I've always liked the descriptive term, Infinite Being, *although you do have to remember that it is no 'a Being' because it is infinite in nature. This concept was emphasized by Lao Tse, author of the* Tao Te Ching, *who said that it is an all-pervasive presence, not a Being in the sense of an individualized deity. Lao Tse went even further and said that to even give this a name brings about a limited perception of something that is really limitless.* Owen K Water

Trees Smile when You Hug Them. Did you know inanimate things feel? When you cut steel there are stress marks on the cut area, but if you dip the steel in ether for a few moments and then cut it there are not stress marks. The cut is perfectly smooth. The steel goes under anesthesia just as we do for surgery. We do not feel the surgery performed.

CHAPTER 13

I PLANNED MY OWN LIFE AND TIME OF DEATH

Why were we created? We all are part of that Infinite Being. Think of yourself as a little molecule in a cell in a body. That body is the Infinite. I like to use this term (Infinite) rather than saying Infinite Being. Infinite Being implies that God is a Being and God is more than a Being. God in Infinite and is everything. There is no name for God and some call it the "Infinite", "UN-named One". Now look down at yourself and look in the mirror. You are part of the Infinite. You are here to live, to observed and to progress back to the Infinite, from which we sprang from. We each are where we are supposed to be right now. You planned your journey here with the help of others and you planned your possible times of death on this earth. We each have approximately five exit points from this earth plane. We are all going though many life times, evolving back to the original Infinite. On a rare occasion an accident may cause a death that was not planned. A disease may set in because of poor eating or drinking habits and cause a premature death. But, on the whole most of the time we cross over at our already set time. Some suicides are planned and some are not. Those that are not planned are the result of many factors. The most prevalent reason is an imbalance of chemicals in the brain, brought on by stress, post traumatic stress syndrome, and some over the anxiety of a life seeming to falling apart. Brain chemistry is very fragile yet more times than not functions rhythmically.

There have been occasions when someone has been able to extend the time of their death. It is as if a new evolutionary step has been taken while living in a present lifetime. So we can rule out destiny. We do have the power to create a longer life if we chose.

In a future book I will reveal how we can change our life with our thoughts.

There are some who through study and understanding, have been able to overcome an illness or condition that seemed impossible to change. There are a few who evolve the ability to heal others and bring about change or healing. I did receive some lessons while on the other side and I am continuing to study to learn more about healing, self and others.

Now that I have totally confused you let me go on to explain more of what I learned. In an angelic vision, Owen K. Water learned this same information: Curiosity. What a word. As we look back over history we realize curiosity spurred people on like Plato, Galileo, Newton, Louis Pasteur, the list goes on.

I have died four times so I would think it is fair to say that the next time I will finally cross over into the Infinite rhelm of Heaven. I hope I am there for quite awhile as this life time has certainly had its ups and downs. There are days I just wish I could go and take it easy. If I were rid of this physical body I would have no pain, fatigue or stress. And then, I look at my life and I do not think I would change anything because I would not be sitting here in the beautiful paradise in Mexico enjoying a new family group that has formed around me. This family is growing and I am still learning. I am also spreading Love and Positive Energy. Many have thanked me for they report that they have received healing and relief because of interaction with me. This is why I am here: to help others find peace and joy. I would not have a beautiful family with grandchildren.

When we begin our life we first have curiosity. Curiosity sets the thought in our mind and then the subconscious takes it and makes it come to fruition. Thus as a god you create whatever you hold in your thoughts or what you dwell upon. I have had times when I was filled with negative thoughts and negative things happened to me. Now I dwell on positive things and wonderful things are happening in my life.

And you thought things happened to you by chance. We create our reality. When we are preparing to come to this side of the veil or shall I say into the earth plane, our subconscious mind is part of our spiritual side (Our Creation) which takes literally whatever you feed it. What we dwell on comes to our reality. A word of caution: Our subconscious mind does not recognize the word "Not" or "No". Any statement you say with a not or no in it will be accepted by the subconscious as a happening. I will give an example. When I say, "I am not going to get a cold". The subconscious hears I am going to get a cold. If this phrase is repeated over and over, well you get the idea.

I worked with a young nurse years ago in a hospital. She was a beautiful girl and I told her many times that she should be in movies. She had a fear of riding the elevator at the two story hospital. She told me she had a fear of being raped on that elevator. I talked to her about her fear and explained how we create our reality. I tried to teach her new things to say to her subconscious mind. A couple of months later she was brought into our emergency room. A man had broken into her apartment and raped her. He left her for dead but she did survive. When she came back to work she did ask my help in setting up new affirmations to say to herself. As you can imagine we all were so sad for her.

We must not forget that in our plans to be born into this world, some of us plan to have a disease or aliment which needs attention. This is usually to help someone else in their journey through this lifetime of learning and to help in our journey back to the Infinite. We must not forget that some come into this world because they want to help and change the outcomes of disease and ailments. It then stands to reason that some will choose to have an ailment to help others learn to find changes and cures.

One example is my late husband. We both signed up to have our bodies donated to science upon our death. When Joe died November 27, 2005, his body went to a Medical School.

The instructions were to return his ashes to my daughter when they completed what they needed to do. They said his remains (ashes) would probably be ready in about two months or less.

Joe was cremated March 31, 2006. The department that used Joe for science apologized to me for taking so long to return his remains but they thought they had a good reason. Usually the bodies they get are in poor shape from very old age or from alcoholism. Because Joe's veins were in such good condition, despite his diabetes, they were able to use a newly developed technique to practice and teach to other surgeons on the smallest veins in the body. Surgeons from around the world got involve and great progress was achieved in the science of tiny vein surgery. I have to say one of Joe's biggest accomplishments happened at this time. Maybe one of your great-great niece or nephew may benefit from this technology because Joe chose to live this life and donate his body.

I cannot repeat this too many times. We all are where we are supposed to be right now. We are here to learn to become self aware. Not aware of my body but of my spirit which is a part of the Infinite. Your personal thinking and spirituality are yours and at the level you are supposed to be in your relationships.

We create our life by our thoughts. There are many sources available to help one learn positive sentences, phrases and affirmations. I advise you to find the ones that fit you.

Some of my affirmations are: 'Every day in every way I am getting better and better'. Emile Coue, 'I Love Myself', 'I am beautiful', 'I am Joy', 'I am healing'. I did learn we all have the ability to heal ourselves and others with meditations and prayers as long as we do it with total Love. There are some conditions that do require medications because we have not evolved enough to eradicate the condition. I like this short cut to healing when I am in a pinch. The Emotional Freedom Technique, or EFT, is the psychological acupressure technique. I am trying to do this more often. You can go to You Tube and type in 'tapping EFT or find EFT' on a search engine or in books from a library.

'I Am Love'. It is important to use this one as often as you can. Love is the most powerful force in the Universe. It is the fastest moving in the entire universe. Physics has proven that when a pair of electrons is separated to different places on earth and one is bounced the other one will immediately reflect by taking the same action as the first. This movement is instantaneous not light speed. Light speed is actually quite slow compared to thought speed.

'I Forgive'. Oh! This one is so powerful. I must first forgive myself before I can forgive others. Sometimes I say 'I Am Forgiveness". I still after years of meditation have times when I reflect on some negatives when others have been cruel to me. I then bounce back with, I Forgive. As time passes I have less and less times of thinking of the negatives in my past.

Each morning I wake up I first say, "Thank You", to "Infinite". I learned this from Wayne Dyer. He has many books that give us some of the best affirmations around. I feel like the sun is shining on my face when I use this one. Thank You. Another person with wonderful affirmations is Louise Hay. She can be found easily by searching her name on a search engine on line. She has many books available. You may go to her site at Hay House.

I learned much about the power of prayer: We have the ability to help others long distance. A few years ago I went to bed and was unable to sleep. I was in Hancock, New Mexico and my daughter was in Washington State. I had a feeling of doom about my daughter. Instead of lamenting I began to meditate and I sent Love in a constant stream for a long time. I don't know how long this process took place but I do know it was over an hour. Around four AM, the telephone woke me. It was my daughter. She was sitting in a police station giving a description of a man who robbed her. She was fine and she stated she was amazed at how calm she remained. She was working at a convenience store on the night shift. I told her about my strong feelings and my prayers for her. There was a long pause before she spoke.

"I am so glad you prayed for me Mom," she said. "I did not get flustered and I even offered the man some food and a drink. At one point he even lay his gun down on the display case but then picked it up when he left."

A couple of weeks later she called me again. "Mom. You are not going to believe what just happened. I received a phone call and it was the man who robbed me. He told me that the store owners should be proud to have me as an employee because I was so nice and did such a good job. He told me that his intention was to kill me so I could not identify him but he just could not do it." This shows the power of Love and prayers and meditation.

I would like to add a thought: it is wise to pray for people who have passed on to the other side, or heaven side. We have no idea what state they are in when they get there. Will they need a period of cleansing and nurturing? Will they be in a cocoon like isolation? The prayers help break down those cocoons (or cloudy fog) with love so they can then join everyone and fully enjoy the Loving Light of the I AM. I had a feeling that the isolation of the cloudy cocoons was a comparison of what purgatory is as mentioned in the Roman Catholic Church.

I found this in the online version
of the Catholic encyclopedia.

Purgatory (Lat., "purgare" {et al}, to make clean, to purify) in accordance with Catholic teaching is a place or condition of temporal punishment for those who, departing this life in God's grace, are, not entirely free from venial faults, or have not fully paid the satisfaction due to their transgressions.

It would be fare to guess that those who harm others could be in cocoons. However,I would not presume be a judge of that. When I was working at a Corrections hospital in, we had a man dying from cancer. His death was a slow unpleasant one. A nurse's job is to help the sick and help relieve pain. Many of the nurses would not immediately respond to his plea for help. I ask one nurse why? She said she was surprised I did not recognize him. She said years before he had killed young boys and ate them. I gasped. Did you just gasp? I would be surprised if you didn't? Do you feel those nurses were doing the right thing by withholding his medications? Do you think he deserved to suffer? At the first moment I felt the same and then my nursing side took over and I took his narcotic to him. It was not my place to pass judgment and inflict punishment. Again I said to myself 'I am forgiveness. I am love".

Why did this man do such gruesome acts? I don't know. Wayne Dyer says it is an act of walking away from God. Those who prosper and do well are walking toward God.

Who do you think will punish this prisoner? It is not God. It is the prisoner himself. What he has done he will suffer for by his own thoughts. Also lack of feeling remorse will often deliver a person into a cocoon. He died in his cell while I was working there. It was difficult but I did mentally send him a prayer.

If there is a hell, I did not see it. I can only say that being in one of the very dark cocoons is akin to hell. To be in an existence of total isolation without contact with anyone but your own thoughts would be maddening. As a nurse in prisons I do know the effects of isolation on some. It is not a pretty picture to watch happen. There are a high percentage of suicides in the isolation community.

When we all sprang forth from that first explosion (We like to call it the Big Bang) of the Infinite of curiosity, the question was what can I experience and how can I return to myself with all the new experiences and knowledge. "I" is used here in the context of The Infinite and of myself just as you use the "I" for yourself. You and I are part of the pure Light and energy that sprang forth in the Big Bang. We were of the Infinite, within the Infinite always. We have evolved though billions of years. I have often read and heard 'We are star dust', and 'We share molecules and electrons with all around us". Quantum physics shows us this is true and nothing is absolutely still. Even granite is in constant motion on the electron level. As I sit here writing a beautiful bouquet of flowers in a blue vase are all sharing electrons with me.

What a wonderful motivation this can be for living our lives... to express that Divine, original feeling as a desire to learn something new every day or, why not...*lots* of new things everyday!

What a beautiful feeling of expansion we can experience by following our innermost fundamental motivation to explore life and become more of what we really are. We are observers. We are part of the divine, watching and experiencing everything. Our potential is infinite, as is the nature of Infinite Being.

Curiosity is the natural drive that will lead us forward along the path to our spiritual home. Parts of this was taken from, Owen K Waters, Spiritual Dynamics http://www.spiritualdynamics.net/. I wish to thank Owen K Waters for permission to use his quotes in this book. As I promised him, I do recommend that you sign up for his newsletter.

CHAPTER 14

WE ARE THE "I AM"

I AM, the newest children book by Dr. Wayne W. Dyer, is taken from his latest book for adults, *Wishes Fulfilled. I AM* teaches children a simple but profound message: God is not far off in the distance, or even merely beside us. In other words, we are not separate from God-we are God!

So far we have learned that in Creation, Curiosity was the first seed of action.

From the I AM, Curiosity it seems, lead to the original consciousness of God, Source, Allah or Infinite Being, Great Grandfather, whatever term you choose to use, that in the seemingly chaotic blast to explore what would happen by watching itself from all different points of view. No thoughts, feelings or emotion was in this initial Big Bang. It simply was Curiosity. What experiences could Infinite observe? Yet! There was a plan, a Divine Plan.

As the stardust collided and eventually formed stars and planets and all celestial bodies continued to form the elements and all that formed the Universe. Let us move to our own planet. Millions of years of turmoil formed this planet and a wonderful thing happened and water happened. Water and land separated from each other. We were just the right distance from our sun and over time life began to form. All of this was the Infinite experiencing and observing. Was I at one point a drop of water in the oceans? It could be: Or an amoeba in the ocean? Why not? Was I cycling back and forth between Heaven and Earth? Yes and I am not sure how many times. Was I ever a dinosaur or a big sloth? Does it matter? I know I am here at this desk writing the story of my near-death-experiences (NDE) mainly because my last NDE I was told I had to come back and tell my stories. There are too many who fear death, who need to learn they are part of GOD. I even know I have more books to write as my connection with the higher realms speaks to me. There will be a second edition in the future as the memories of what I experienced while I was on the other side of the Veil come to me. The older some of us are the more memories come and our mind. I am in awe of the splendor of the memories.

But I digress. Today we all are those viewpoints of the Infinite. We each are part of the Infinite in our life that we are living now. Forget about the other lives because they will take care of themselves. Everything in the Universe is conscious in one form or another. My right, small toe is a part of me and I would like to keep it. Just as my heart is part of me along with a cell in my knee. All of these things are part of me. So we are all part of God. We are part of/and God the Infinite. I always feel a little cozy and fuzzy when I think of it this way. So I find myself thanking my body parts for functioning well and giving me a good life, even when I hurt. The hurt will pass. The pain is part of my observation. By overeating in the past I am over weight and so my back and knees hurt. I am slowly losing weight and my back and knees are becoming a little less painful. I did have polio when I was little and that too has added to my pain. I have been able to reduce that pain tremendously with my thoughts and actions. I try to steer clear of negative talk. I will go into detail in another book about the lengths I went to when I was in a wheelchair when I was told I would be in for the rest of my life yet in July 2005 I got out of that wheel chair for the last time.

Consciousness was the only tool Infinite Being had with which to create the universe, everything is made of consciousness. Owen K Waters from "Discover Your Sacred Purpose In Life" http://www.spiritualdynamics.net/ He too is here to teach us and help mankind climb to higher levels of consciousness. I am grateful for the validation I received because of what I learned. The same information was made available to Owen Waters in such a beautiful encounter.

Curiosity was the original motivation in Creation so it is your most divine inherent quality. At one point when the Infinite was curious, it stands to reason that it led to the act of Creation. So the decision was to be a Creator.

I Remember the teacher who was giving us these lessons as I sat on the bench was careful to make it easy to understand. When we use the attribute of creativity we search for a solution to a challenge. This even preceded the act of figuring out how to make Creation possible. The most fundamental attributes of human consciousness are curiosity followed by creativity. We are created in the image of the Creator because we are a part of the Creator.

I remember a time when I was about eight years old and my father was trying to load a plow onto his pickup truck. He struggled for a long time. I watched and thought 'what would make loading the plow easier?' My curiosity led to creativity. I thought of a possible solution. I went over to Dad's work shop and picked up two, two-by-four boards and dragged them to the pickup and placed one on the tailgate. The look on my father's face was the best gift I had ever received from him. He put the other board on the edge of the tailgate and easily pushed the plow up into the bed of the truck. He then ran into the house and told my mother what I had done: that was probably one of the best moments of my childhood. I glowed with pride. My father had given me credit for my creativity. It is OK to be happy and proud of solving a problem.

We each are right where we are supposed to be. You are at the level of understanding you are supposed to be. You are in the religion you are supposed to be as long as we are advocates of love for all. We are all on a different level of enlightenment. It all depends on our point of evolution. The higher levels of creativity are now budding as we see advances in technology at a dizzying rate.

I was shown a bit concerning the dynamics of creation which would come forth at a high level of mathematical genius and quantum physics. I think we can leave that to the experts. I was unable to understand it but the fact remains, there is a grand logical scheme in the creation. It was not just a big bang that haphazardly happened. Trillions of years have passed since the first creation.

I got the impression this was not the first time the universe was formed. I do not know if there are other universes or how many times creation happened. I do know it was more than this present time. I certainly would not want to speculate. I am only telling you what I learned. Much of it I did not understand but my level of understanding is limited to where I am at this moment.

When I was sixteen, I had trouble understanding God is everything, even the sand, rocks, air, space, and all that is that is visible and invisible. Now at the age of 70 I can grasp the concept more easily.

We all are observers and experiencing at the same time as part of the whole (GOD/S). After the supposed chaos of the first few million years each of us require time for planning before we resume another life time in a physical realm. At first we would quickly make a few plans together in groups and then cross over to birth on earth. As a few thousand years passed we learned to slow down and plan more thoughtfully in order to return to the beautiful bliss of being totally one with God. Teachers have joined us at different times to help us understand and complete our goal in the present lifetime. We do have helpers from the other side (heaven if you will), who do their part in urging us into the right direction.

I am now living in a place I call Paradise in Mexico. Flowers bloom year round and the temperatures never get too hot for very long. We do not need an air conditioner but we do use a little area heater during three winter months. I am now finishing this book in February 2015 around Valentines day. It will be warm enough to go for a nice walk in a few minutes to enjoy the birds, butterflies, sounds and smells. The local people are friendly and very helpful.

I wish to leave you with these thoughts. Since the beginning of time we have tried to understand what or who God is while on the earth or physical side of life. The idea that God is the supreme judge with a heavy fist has been the theme throughout much of history. I learned that we are our own judge. Since we each are part of the Infinite God, when we cross over to the heaven realm we leave this little human ego behind and we become our own judge.

Many have had near death experiences and each one is different, just as everyone has unique fingerprints or each snowflake is different. Reading many accounts of people's experiences gives us a much broader perspective of what Heaven is all about. I know I will be joined by my loved ones and more and a great celebration will pull me into a celestial dance of pure Joy. I am looking forward to that day. I do know that I have more to accomplish on this earth plane in this body made of the physical matter. I would rather complete all the plans I set for myself before I move across the veil in order to be able to move up to the next goals I wish to accomplish. Each life time in the physical is like going to school. We are all learning and experiencing. We are also observers of the Infinite Self. Our goal in this life is to be Love, give out Love and to receive Love. How many times have we heard or seen the words 'God is Love'? We can turn it around and say 'Love is God'. When I look in the mirror I try to remember who I am looking at. When I look at you I try to remember who I am looking at. I am looking at God.

From the Hindu perspective we hear the word Namasté quite often. 'Namaste' or 'namaskar' is the Indian way of greeting each other. Wherever they are – on the street, in the house, in public transport, on vacation or on the phone – when Hindus meet people they know or strangers with whom they want to initiate a conversation, namaste is the customary courtesy greeting to begin with and often to end with. It is not a superficial gesture or a mere word, and is for all people - young and old, friends and strangers.

Namaste and its common variants 'namaskar,' 'namaskaara' or 'namaskaram', is one of the five forms of formal traditional greeting mentioned in the Vedas. This is normally understood as prostration but it actually refers to paying homage or showing respect to one another, as is the practice today, when we greet each other.

Namaste' means: "I honor the place within you where the entire Universe resides; I honor the place within you of love, of light, of truth, of peace; I honor the place within you, where, when you are in that place in you, and I am in that place in me, there is only one of us."

The following words are very close to the original writings.

Genesis 1
New International Version (NIV)
26 Then God said, "Let us make mankind in our image, in our likeness,

Genesis 1 (New King James Version)
26 Then God said, "Let Us make man in Our image, according to Our likeness; let them have dominion over the fish of the sea, over the birds of the air, ~

You noticed that it says Let Us make man in Our Image, according to Our Likeness.

AFTERWORD

While I was a nurse, I was able to help many people face death in peace as I held their hands at or near their death. I have been able to help families be with the dying loved one with more peace and understanding. It did not lessen the grief but I believe the knowledge of what is waiting on the other-side made the grieving less painful. The person who crosses over is with their family on both sides of the veil. Dying we simply step through a veil. At conception we step through the veil.

I continue to bring the message to as many as I can. My last NDE I learned I had to write this down so it can be shared.

If someone crosses over who has not been able to work through actions of abuse to anyone or animal will probably be in need of prayers and meditation by those of us left on this side. Our prayers and meditations are very powerful and have a profound effect on others even on the other side.

I will write another edition of this book at a later date. There is more information that was just too lengthy to put in this easy to read rendition.

Other books will follow including, 'How my blind girl friend found my soul-mate' for me, and some special stories about animals I have encountered that surely had a guiding hand from my angels. I have been pressed into writing a book about how I got myself out of a wheel chair after being told I would never walk again. As I said earlier, I had polio when I was about two years old but soon was over it. I had a wonderfully full life after that even a career as a nurse. I then became weak and soon in a wheelchair. I was diagnosed with Post Polio Syndrome.

I have told so many stories of funny and strange things that happened when I was a nurse that I have been told I need to write those down. I will take it one step at a time and allow my spirit to guide me to each step in the future.

I am living near Lake Chapala, Mexico. In the surrounding towns there is such poverty that I will be putting my money toward helping them with food, clothing, education and refurbishing their housing and land to grow good produce to sell and eat.

Many have had NDE and some tell of the experience of seeing hell. I never saw a hell. I can only relate to what I experienced.

Each person has a slightly different experience so no to reports of a NDE are the same.

You can read little excerpts of others on NDE
http://www.nderf.org/NDERF/NDE_Archives/NDERF_NDEs.htm

http://www.nderf.org/

http://www.nderf.org/index.htm

I learned Why creation happen and how it happened.

Why were we created.

It is easy when one is in spirit surrounded by love and light to say what we are willing to go through on reaching the earth plane but everything we go through is a necessary lesson, for our spiritual development and as soon as you accept that everything that happens is for a reason and the most painful

lessons help us to grow more spiritually, you will find it helps. Acceptance is the key, even when we do not like what is happening. Hard as it usually is!